IDENTIFICATION GUIDES
British & European
Fossils

Publisher and Creative Director: Nick Wells
Project Editor: Sara Robson
Picture Research: Victoria Lyle
Consultant Naturalist: Chris McLaren
Art Director: Mike Spender
Digital Design and Production: Chris Herbert
Layout Design: Theresa Maynard

Special thanks to: Amanda Leigh, Julia Rolf, Claire Walker and Gemma Walters

08 10 12 11 09

1 3 5 7 9 10 8 6 4 2

This edition first published 2008 by
FLAME TREE PUBLISHING
Crabtree Hall, Crabtree Lane
Fulham, London SW6 6TY
United Kingdom

www.flametreepublishing.com

Flame Tree Publishing is part of the Foundry Creative Media Co. Ltd.

ISBN 978-1-84451-934-7

A CIP record for this book is available from the British Library upon request.

Printed in China

IDENTIFICATION GUIDES
British & European
Fossils

H. Gee, C. Fitzsimons
& S. McCormick

FLAME TREE
PUBLISHING

Contents

Introduction

Fossils are the mineralized remains of long-dead animals and plants, and can be beautiful objects as well as fascinating hints of the riotous diversity and profusion of life long ago. This book is intended for those curious about the fossils they pick up on the beach after storms, in road or railway cuttings or in quarries. In it we have described and illustrated many of the most common fossils to be found in Europe, with details of their geological ages and where you can expect to find them. Some of the terms we use to describe the fossils may be unfamiliar, so we have included a glossary (see p. 20) and a chart of the names and relative ages of the geological strata (see Fig. 2 on p. 16 and 17).

Collecting the fossils in one's own neighbourhood can be a rewarding pastime, and palaeontology is one of the few sciences in which the keen amateur can still make a vital contribution. Those in search of more information should contact their local museum, which will be pleased to provide more detailed information than can be squeezed into this identification guide. When setting out on a fossil-hunting expedition, remember that many fossil-bearing localities are dangerous places. Wear heavy boots and a hard hat and, if unaccompanied, tell somebody where you are going and how long you expect to be away. At the site, take careful notes about the fossils and their locations as precisely as you can – this is important scientific information. If possible, take colour photographs. However you store or display your trophies at home, make sure each one has a label recording essential site details, and keep duplicate labels in a card index or on a personal computer. Fossils without information may look pretty but are scientifically useless.

Most importantly of all, **make sure you have written permission from the landowner to collect fossils on the site.** Many sites are on private land or owned by railway companies, quarry operators and so on. Some are protected sites of scientific interest and unauthorized collection may be forbidden. If in doubt, contact your local museum who should have information about local sites of interest.

How to Use this Book

We have divided this book into a number of colour-coded sections reflecting the classification of the animals and plants found as fossils. To identify your fossil, first decide the group to which it belongs using the **Guide to Identification** that follows. It is possible that you will not be able to find the exact fossil in this book, although you will probably find something like it, and get some idea about its broad zoological or botanical affinity.

Guide to Identification

First decide the group to which your fossil belongs.

Plants are hardly ever found complete as fossils, although leaves, fruits and fragments of wood, bark and stems are not uncommon. This makes identification extremely difficult, even for the specialist. Some plants have one Latin name for the leaves, another for the stems, yet a third for the roots. Some are even confused with plantlike animals such as bryozoans or graptolites.

Sponges & Corals: sponges are simple marine animals known from well before the Cambrian period to the present day. Their varied shapes make them hard to identify positively. Their skeletons are made of a meshwork either of protein or of *calcareous* or *siliceous spicules*. These are useful clues to identification but are microscopic and fall outside the skills of most amateurs. **Archaeocyaths** are cup-shaped sponge-like animals known only from the Cambrian. Corals look a bit like sponges but are in fact colonial animals related to sea anemones. The corals preserved as fossils are the remains of the *calcareous* 'cups' secreted by each individual, or polyp. They are classified by the numbers and arrangements of partition walls or septa in each cup.

Molluscs are by far the most important fossil group. Common from the Cambrian to the present day, the snails or **gastropods** have a single shell coiled in a helix or plane spiral. Unlike the cephalopod shell, it is not subdivided internally by septa.

The **bivalve** body is encased in two valves, one on each side, joined along the back by a hinge. First recorded in the Middle Cambrian, they did not really come into their own until the Mesozoic and are abundant today.

 Cephalopods include the modern squid, octopi and nautilus, only the last of which retains an external shell. The cephalopod shell is subdivided internally by septa. Making their first appearance in the Chinese Middle Cambrian, **nautiloids** first appeared in Europe in any numbers in the Lower Ordovician, with **ammonoids** in the Upper Devonian. A tube or *siphuncle* runs down the middle of the nautiloid shell, connecting all the chambers. In ammonoids and one group of nautiloids it runs down one edge. Nautiloid shells usually have simple *suture* lines and, if coiled, a central perforation. Ammonoid shells generally lack this, but their suture lines range from simple zig-zags (in goniatites), zig-zags alternating with more complex *saddles* and *lobes* (ceratites), to very sinuous and complex shapes (ammonites). The rapid evolution, worldwide distribution and characteristic suturing of ammonites makes them superb *zone fossils* in the Mesozoic, especially the Jurassic. They died out in the Cretaceous.

 Arthropods, or joined-limbed animals, are the most abundant animals today and include insects, millipedes, centipedes, crustaceans, spiders, scorpions, mites and ticks. But the most important fossil arthropods are the **trilobites**, which appeared in profusion in the Cambrian and dominated the seas until their decline in the Carboniferous. They are not known after the end of the Permian. More than 1500 *genera* and thousands of species are known from all parts of the world. Rich trilobite pickings can be had in Sweden, Norway, Wales (Cambrian), Scotland (Ordovician), the west of England (Silurian), Russia, Bohemia, and parts of North Africa and North America. The trilobite body ranges in length from less than a millimetre to more than 75 centimetres, and is divided lengthwise into a head, *thorax* and tail, and sideways into three lobes (hence the name) like the nave and aisles of a church. The head has a central lobe or *glabella* with or without a pair of compound eyes, one on each side, and a front margin, sometimes extending towards the *genal angles* on the rear corners of the head.

 Bryozoa or 'moss animals' are exclusively colonial and are easily confused with corals and some kinds of graptolite. Important as fossils, they are usually found as low-growing patterns or encrustations on rock surfaces, but may form erect, branching colonies. Each cup or *theca* housed a tiny individual or *zooid*. There are four major groups of bryozoa: the **trepostomes, cryptostomes, cheilostomes** and **cyclostomes**. All are represented here but precise details of identification usually require the help of a specialist.

 Brachiopods are marine animals with two distinct but equilateral valves; a lower *pedicle valve* (usually the larger of the two) and an upper, *brachial valve*. The shells of the unrelated bivalve molluscs, in contrast, are lateral (left and right, rather than top and bottom) and are not usually equilateral. Living brachiopods attach themselves to a solid object by a fleshy stalk or *pedicle* emerging from the back of the shell; the *gape* is always at the front rather than underneath, as in bivalves. The animals feed by trapping particles in a coiled arrangement of tentacles called a *lophophore*, which is supported by a skeleton or *brachidium* that is sometimes preserved in fossils in various shapes than can aid identification; it may be arranged as a pair of simple 'horns' or *crura*, or in delicate spiral shapes. There are two major groups of brachiopod, the **inarticulates** with *chitinous* or *calcareous* valves held together by soft tissues; and the **articulates**, with *calcareous* valves hinged together by two teeth in the pedicle valve that fit into two sockets in the brachial valve. The hinge may run along the entire back edge of the brachial valve (*strophic*) or just pivot on a small part of it just under the beak, like the silver lid in an antique wine decanter (*non-strophic*). The space between the beak and the hinge line is called the *interarea*; the gap in the pedicle valve between the hinge and the place where the pedicle emerges (the *pedicle foramen*) is called the *delthyrium*, and may be closed by a pair of small plates. The articulates comprise several important subgroups, the orthids, strophomenids, pentamerids, spiriferids, rhynchonellids and terebratulids, all of which are common as fossils. Fewer than 100 of the 3,000 recorded genera of brachiopods survive today.

Echinoderms, the spiny-skinned animals, have been important in the sea since the Lower Cambrian. Modern forms include starfish (asteroids), brittle-stars (ophiuroids), sea-urchins (echinoids), sea-cucumbers (holothurians) and sea-lilies and feather-stars (crinoids), although many other strange groups such as cystoids and blastoids have come and gone. All usually have a skeleton of calcite plates and a distinctive five-way symmetry, as well as a distinctive system of water tubes connected to mobile 'tube feet' arranged along a series of food grooves. The **crinoids** or sea-lilies are rare today but are very important as fossils from the Lower Ordovician upwards. The fragile **asteroids** and **ophiuroids** are generally rare as fossils but are locally abundant if conditions of preservation are just right.

Graptolites were marine animals that lived in colonies made of a kind of protein, preserved in rocks as a black carbon film; they get their name from their resemblance to pencil markings. Each individual or *zooid* lived in a cup or *theca*, arranged in lines along one (*uniserial*) or both (*biserial*) sides of the blade-like *stipe*. There were two principal groups of graptolite: the bushy bottom-living **dendroids**, first to evolve in the mid-Cambrian and last to die out, in the late Carboniferous; and the free-floating **graptoloids**, common in the Ordovician, Silurian and lower Devonian. The graptoloids were very diverse and are extremely useful as *zone fossils* in the Ordovician and Silurian.

The **vertebrates**, or backboned animals, comprise the fishes, amphibians, reptiles, birds and mammals, including ourselves. Although the very earliest fishes appeared in the Late Cambrian, the fossil record of vertebrates is generally rather poor. Unless armoured with bony plates or scales, the bony skeleton of vertebrates is internal and tends to break up easily after death. For all that one hears and reads about dinosaurs, the most common (or least rare) vertebrate fossils are teeth. These are coated with enamel, the hardest substance produced by living organisms, and are thus resistant to damage. The rarest vertebrate species of all is our own, usually betrayed only by signs of activity, such as stone tools, rather than bones.

Making a Positive Identification

The fossils are organized into several colour-coded sections, marked by symbols for each major group. Once you have found the right page, you will find details of the characteristic features of each fossil described in the first paragraph, under **Primary Identification Features**, and notes on the stratigraphic position (see Fig. 2 on p. 16 and 17) and geographical distribution in the second paragraph. More information about the evolution of the fossil form and its relatives can be found in the third paragraph, under **Additional Information**, whereas the fourth paragraph, **Similar Forms**, lists fossils that either look similar or may be related to the fossil in the main picture (see Fig. 1 on p. 15). Some pages illustrate a variety of common but related fossil forms.

How Fossils Form

Far from being the actual remains of animals and plants that lived millions of years ago, fossils are impressions left when the dead bodies of creatures fell into sand, mud, volcanic ash or other soft materials and rotted away, leaving a hole which became filled with minerals percolating through the sediment. Millions of years of slow accumulation squeezed the soft sediment into rocks such as sandstone, limestone and shale. Animals with hard shells fossilize the best, and the best places to find fossils are sediments that formed on the seafloor. So the most common fossils are hard-shelled marine animals such as trilobites and molluscs. The rarest of all are backboned animals that lived on land, such as fossil **hominids**.

Specimen Spread

Genus of Fossil

Symbol donates
type of Fossil

Colour illustration
of characteristics

FIG. 1

Colour
denotes
type of Fossil

Name of
subgroup

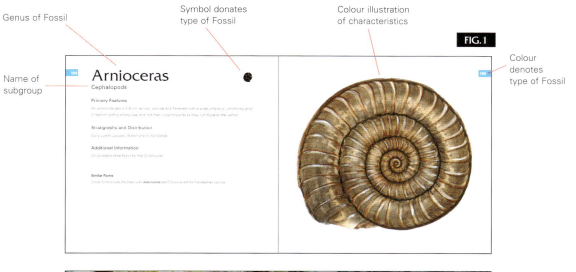

Arnioceras
Cephalopods

Primary Features

An ammonite about 5-6 cm across, evolute and flattened with a wide umbilicus, whorls square in section with a strong keel and ribs that curve forwards as they run towards the center.

Stratigraphy and Distribution

Early Lower Jurassic (Sinemurian). Worldwide.

Additional Information

An excellent zone fossil for the Sinemurian.

Similar Forms

Similar forms include the Sinemurian *Asteroceras* and *Euasteras* and the Pliensbachian *Liparoceras*.

Colour photo
offering an
alternative
view of
the Fossil

Arnioceras lives from the Early Lower Jurassic period and are found worldwide.

Time Chart

Era	Period		Stage	Age
Cenozoic	**Quaternary**		Holocene (Recent) Pleistocene	
				2
	Tertiary		Pliocene Miocene Oligocene Eocene Palaeocene	
				65
Mesozoic	**Cretaceous**		Maastrichtian Senonian Turonian Cenomanian Albian Aptian Neocomian: Barremian Hauterivian Valanginian Berriasian	
				135
	Jurassic		Portlandian/Volgian Kimmeridgian Oxfordian Callovian Bathonian Bajocian Lias: Toarcian Pliensbachian Sinemurian Hettangian	
				200
	Triassic			
				240

FIG.2

17

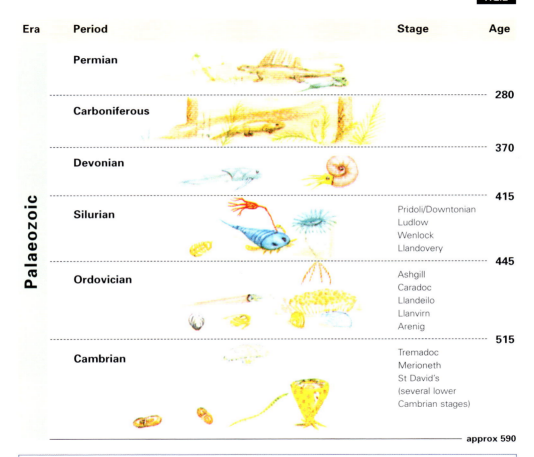

Era	Period	Stage	Age
Palaeozoic	Permian		
			280
	Carboniferous		
			370
	Devonian		
			415
	Silurian	Pridoli/Downtonian Ludlow Wenlock Llandovery	
			445
	Ordovician	Ashgill Caradoc Llandeilo Llanvirn Arenig	
			515
	Cambrian	Tremadoc Merioneth St David's (several lower Cambrian stages)	
			approx 590

Ages in the time chart are given in millions of years and are approximate.

Names and numbers of stages in each period are likely to vary from place to place.

Where Fossils are Found

This approximate map outlines the basic features of European geology, illustrating the locations of the major sedimentary sequences.

FIG.3

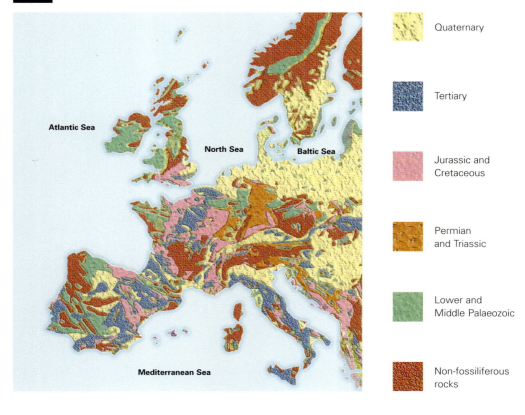

Quaternary

Tertiary

Jurassic and Cretaceous

Permian and Triassic

Lower and Middle Palaeozoic

Non-fossiliferous rocks

Glossary of Terms

Aperture
The main opening in the gastropod or cephalopod shell through which the animal meets the exterior.

Axis
The central, longitudinal lobe of a trilobite.

Beak
The convex protrusion of a brachiopod (or bivalve) valve behind (or above) the hinge.

Biconical
The shape of two cones joined together at the base.

Biserial
Arrangement in graptolites whereby thecae occupy both sides of a single stipe.

Brachial valve
The upper, often smaller, valve of a brachiopod.

Brachidium
Skeleton that supports the brachiopod lophophore.

Calcareous
Made of calcium carbonate or calcite.

Calyx
The body or theca of a crinoid.

Chiton/Chitinous
A hard fibrous protein which makes up the hard external skeleton of insects and some other animals.

Chondrophore
Attachment for shell-closing muscles in some bivalves such as *Mya* that lack hinge teeth.

Cirri
Spiny outgrowths from the crinoid stem.

Convolute
Style of shell coiling in which the inner whorls are partly (but not completely) obscured by the last whorl.

Crura
Horn-shaped processes of the brachidium in brachiopods.

Delthyrium
Part of the brachiopod pedicle valve between the pedicle foramen and the hinge. May have its own plates.

Evolute
Style of shell coiling in which all the whorls are exposed.

Facial sutures
Junctions between the plates on the trilobite head.

Form genus
A genus used for the convenient reference of distinctive forms in cases where evolutionary relationship is obscure, as is sometimes the case with plants and graptolites.

Front border
Border at the front of the trilobite head.

Gape
The opening in a shell opposite the hinge.

Genal angles
The angles of the rear, outermost corners of the trilobite head.

Genal spines
Spines that grow from the genal angles.

Genus
(pl. Genera) A group of species thought to have close affinity in appearance or evolutionary relationship. The first (upper-case initial) name in a formal zoological or botanical name, e.g. *Genus species*. Genera make more convenient taxonomic units than species in palaeontology.

Glabella
The central, often lobed part of the trilobite head.

Interarea
Part of the brachiopod shell between hinge and beak.

Involute
Style of shell coiling in which the last whorl obscures all the other whorls.

Keel
The outer edge of an ammonite shell.

Last whorl
The main, youngest whorl of a gastropod shell, next to the aperture.

Lobe

Loop in an ammonoid suture line that points backwards, i.e. away from the aperture.

Lophophore

Organ of ciliated tentacles in brachiopods and some other animals.

Non-Strophic

Condition of the hinge in brachiopods in which it does not occupy the width of the back edge of the brachial valve.

Pedicle

The fleshy stalk of a brachiopod.

Pedicle foramen

The hole in the brachiopod pedicle valve through which the pedicle protrudes.

Pedicle valve

The lower and often the larger of the brachiopod valves.

Planispiral

Style of coiling in which the whorls form a flat disc rather than a helical shape.

Polyp

A single individual in a coral colony.

Protoconch

The smallest, embryonic shell compartment or whorl in a cephalopod or gastropod shell.

Saddle

Loop in an ammonoid suture line that points forwards, i.e. towards the aperture.

Septa

Internal partitions in a coral cup or cephalopod shell (singular: septum).

Siliceous

Made of the mineral silica, a compound of silicon and oxygen found in the spicules of some sponges.

Siphuncle

The tube running through the middle of the nautiloid shell, or along one edge of the ammonoid shell, that links the compartments.

Slit band

A line of ornament in some early gastropods left by the overgrowth of a slit in the edges of successive whorls.

Species

A kind or type of animal or plant referred to by the second (lower-case) name in a formal zoological or botanical name, e.g. *Genus species*.

Spicules
Microscopic skeletal elements of a sponge.

Spire
Part of the gastropod shell that excludes the last whorl.

Stipe
The main stem or stalk of a graptolite.

Stratigraphy
The science of ordering successive layers or strata of sedimentary rocks into a sequence that reflects relative age.

Strophic
Condition of the hinge in brachiopods in which it occupies the entire width of the back edge of the brachial valve.

Suture
Superficial line marking the junction of plates in the trilobite head or shell compartments in cephalopods.

Theca
The cup housing a graptolite zooid; the body of a crinoid, cystoid, blastoid or (conventionally) a calcihordate echinoderm.

Thorax
The trunk; the segmented part of an arthropod (and trilobite) body between the head and the tail.

Umbilicus
The central hollow in the sides of a cephalopod shell or the base of a gastropod shell.

Valve
One of the pair of shells in brachiopods or bivalves.

Venter
The lower edge of an ammonoid shell below the aperture.

Zone fossil
A fossil with a wide distribution but limited stratigraphic range that can, because of these attributes, be used to judge the age of the rocks in which it occurs.

Zooid An individual member of a colonial organism such as a graptolite or bryozoan.

Ammonoid

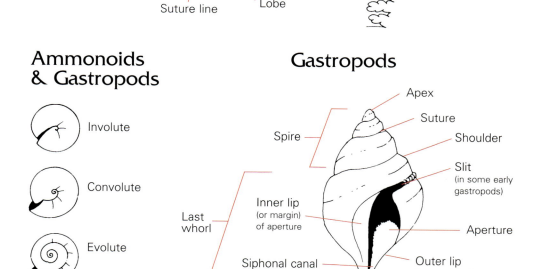

Venter

Keel

Umbilicus

Aperture

Saddle

Suture line

Lobe

Suturing in goniatites

Suturing in ceratites

Suturing in ammonites

Ammonoids & Gastropods

Involute

Convolute

Evolute

Gastropods

Apex

Suture

Shoulder

Spire

Slit
(in some early gastropods)

Last whorl

Inner lip
(or margin)
of aperture

Aperture

Siphonal canal

Outer lip
(or margin) of aperture

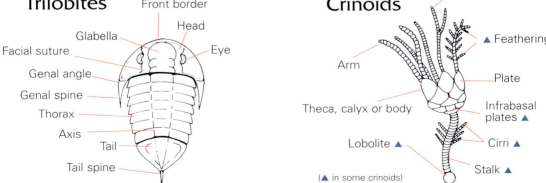

Bivalves

Hinge
Valve
Beak
Growth line
Rib
Tooth
Front end
Hind end

Brachiopods

Beak
Pedicle foramen
Interarea
Delthyrium
Pedicle valve
Hinge
Brachial valve
Radial ridge
Gape (front edge)

Graptolites

Thecae (each one housing a zooid)
Uniserial form
Stipe
Biserial form

Trilobites

Front border
Head
Glabella
Eye
Facial suture
Genal angle
Genal spine
Thorax
Axis
Tail
Tail spine

Crinoids

▲ Branching arm
▲ Feathering
Arm
Plate
Theca, calyx or body
Infrabasal plates ▲
Lobolite ▲
Cirri ▲
Stalk ▲
(▲ in some crinoids)

Rhynia
Psilophytales

Primary Features

Rhynia (**1**) had prostrate, woody stems a few centimetres long from which grew branching stalks, each one terminating in a sporangium or spore capsule. Compare with *Zosterophyllum* (**2**).

Stratigraphy and Distribution

Rhynia comes from the Lower Devonian of Scotland. Psilophytales ranged from the Silurian to the Devonian, although there are fossil hints of still earlier plants.

Additional Information

Psilophytales were the earliest definitely known land plants. They had no proper roots or leaves and probably lived on tidal flats not far from the sea.

Similar Forms

Tiny *Cooksonia* (2–4 cm tall, Silurian) is the earliest known land plant; *Zosterophyllum* (Lower Devonian) had sporangia arranged on short side-branches. Other forms include the brush-like *Asterophyllum*.

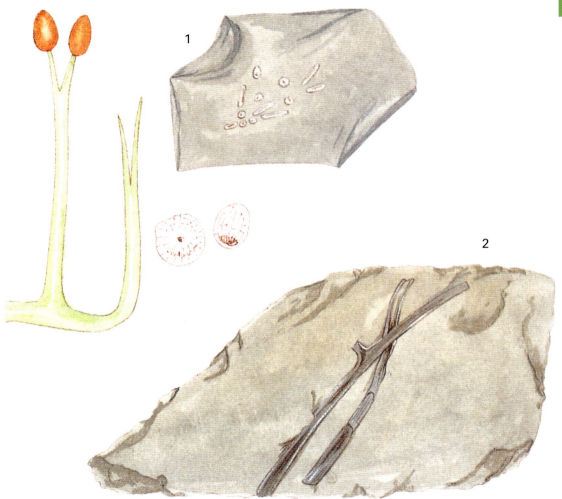

Lepidodendron
Clubmosses

Primary Features

Narrow branches with needle-like leaves grew from the top of a single trunk. The bark is patterned with the lens-shaped scars of old leaf-bases (**1**), arranged spirally around the trunk.

Stratigraphy and Distribution

Lower Carboniferous (Coal Measures) of Europe and North America.

Additional Information

Modern clubmosses such as *Selaginella* are small, but Carboniferous forms such as *Lepidodendron* grew to 30 m in height and were important swamp forest trees.

Similar Forms

The bark of the contemporary *Sigillaria* (**2**), is patterned in straight, vertical rows of circles rather than lens-shapes.

Roots of *Stigmaria* are patterned with holes arranged like the buttons in a Chesterfield sofa.

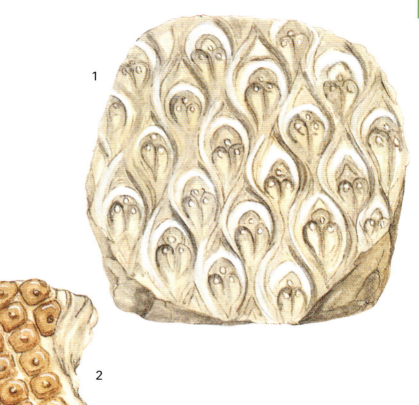

1

2

Lepidodendron is a scale-like fossil that is actually the bark of a clubmoss that grew in hot and humid swampland.

Calamites

Horsetails

Primary Features

The tree-sized (up to 30 m) *Calamites* stems are found as internal casts (**1**) with vertical ribbing and horizontal joints from which branches grew. *Annularia* (**2**) represents the rosettes of leaves from *Calamites* or a close relative.

Stratigraphy and Distribution

Lower Carboniferous (Coal Measures) of Europe and North America.

Additional Information

Horsetails range from the Devonian to the small *Equisetum* of the present day. The stems are not woody, but contain pith; reproduction is from spore-bearing cones.

Similar Forms

Several kinds of horsetails grew in the Carboniferous, known from stems, leaves and roots.

Asterophyllites is like *Annularia* but about one-third the size.

1

2

Calamites are extinct segmented plants similar to today's horsetail. Fossils are casts of the central cylinder of the trunk.

Neuropteris
Seed Ferns

Primary Features

Large frond-like leaves (**1**) radiating in pairs from a central axis. *Neuropteris* is a 'form' genus, known only from its leaves.

Stratigraphy and Distribution

Carboniferous (Coal Measures) of Europe and North America. Seed ferns range from the mid-Devonian to the Upper Permian.

Additional Information

Seed ferns looked like true ferns but were woody plants that grew to the size of large trees. Instead of spores they bore large, egg-shaped seeds.

Similar Forms

Seed fern and true fern fronds look so similar that it is hard to tell the difference without the seeds.

Cyclopteris (**2**) has large, oval leaves; *Medullosa* is a commonly found seed fern.

Other ferns or seed ferns include *Sphenopteris* and *Pecopteris*.

1

2

Neuropteris were seed ferns, which were amongst the earliest seed-bearing plants on the planet.

Cordaites
Cordaitales

Primary Features

Trees with long (more than 30 cm), parallel-veined ribbon- or strap-like leaves (*Cordaites*, **1**) and large conifer-like cones (*Cordaianthus*, **2**).

Stratigraphy and Distribution

Although *Cordaites* itself is known from the Carboniferous to the Permian, the Cordaitales in general ranged from Devonian to Triassic times.

Additional Information

The Cordaitales bore seeds in large cones and may have included the ancestors of modern conifers.

Similar Forms

None.

Ginkgo
Ginkgoales

Primary Features

Distinctive bilobed leaves 2–5 cm across, reminiscent of fig leaves.

Stratigraphy and Distribution

Relatively common in Mesozoic rocks from around the world.

Additional Information

The Ginkgoales are related to conifers, although they are deciduous with broad leaves rather than needles. They range from the Devonian to the single living form *Ginkgo biloba*.

Similar Forms

Several forms of Ginkgo are known. The leaves of *Ginkgo huttoni* (illustrated) from the Lower Middle Jurassic are dissected, but those of others such as *G. digitata* were fan-shaped.

The present day Ginkgo plants are known as living fossils as their relatives have existed for over 200 million years.

Pterophyllum
Bennettitales

Primary Features

Delicate fern-like fronds. The narrow leaflets have rather square ends and are attached to a relatively broad, veined axis.

Stratigraphy and Distribution

Triassic and Jurassic rocks from around the world.

Additional Information

Bennettitales were conifer-like trees with feathery leaves, thick cycad-like trunks and unusual flower-like reproductive organs. Range from Carboniferous to Cretaceous.

Similar Forms

Leaves easily confused with ferns (although seed ferns such as *Neuropteris* were extinct by the Mesozoic), or the closely related seed-bearing Nilssonales (Mesozoic). The large 'flowers' look like nothing else, except possibly sea-urchin tests!

Pterophyllum can be found in Triassic and Jurassic rocks around the world.

Cephalotaxus

Conifers

Primary Features

These needles of *Cephalotaxus* (**1**), 25 mm long, and cone of *Doliostrobus* (**2**), 15 mm tall, come from conifers of the yew family.

Stratigraphy and Distribution

These specimens come from the Eocene oil shales of Messel, Germany, although conifers and their relatives are known from the Carboniferous onwards.

Additional Information

Other fossils include needles and cones of the monkey-puzzle *Araucaria* (Jurassic-Recent) and the redwoods *Sequoia* (Miocene/Recent) and *Sequoiadendron* (Oligocene).

Similar Forms

Bennettitales, cycads, cordaites (**Cordaitanthus**).

Flowering Plants
Angiosperms

Primary Features

Leaves of poplar *Populus* (**1**, Cretaceous-Recent) and maple *Acer* (**2**, Palaeocene-Recent) are typical angiosperm remains. Pleistocene hazelnut shells (**3**, *Corylus*) show evidence of rodent gnawing.

Stratigraphy and Distribution

Angiosperms are found worldwide and dominate floras from the Cretaceous onwards.
Early forms such as willow and magnolia still thrive today.

Additional Information

The evolution of flowering plants was arguably the greatest revolution in life in the past 100 million years. Fossil leaves look little different from modern ones.

Similar Forms

Ginkgo, some conifers.

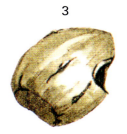

A Populus fossil of a poplar leaf.

Fossil Wood

Primary Features

Fossil wood (such as oak *Quercus*, illustrated) is common in some places, occasionally as entire tree-trunks. It is more often found as highly polished sections in fossil shops.

Stratigraphy and Distribution

Fossil wood from angiosperms is known from the Cretaceous onwards, although wood from other plants is also known.

Additional Information

Although the best fossil wood comes from semi-arid environments, it is known from a variety of settings such as coal swamps, peat bogs and so on.

Similar Forms

The wood from a wide variety of plants ranging from **Lepidodendron** upwards has been found, from small fragments to whole trunks with roots attached. Perhaps the earliest examples are trunks of the enigmatic Devonian 'nematophyte' plant *Prototaxites*, up to 1 m across and several metres long.

Fossil wood, from the petrified forest in the Arizona desert, USA.

Archaeocyaths

Primary Features

Cup-shaped (up to 10 cm tall), with double walls separated by simple partitions (*Regulares*) or a complicated labyrinthine network (*Irregulares*). Often found preserved in section, as shown here.

Stratigraphy and Distribution

Lower Cambrian, more rarely Middle Cambrian of Normandy, Sardinia, southern Spain, parts of north Africa, eastern Eurasia and North America.

Additional Information

Archaeocyaths were sponge-like marine organisms that evolved and became extinct in the Cambrian. They were the first reef-building animals.

Similar Forms

Corals, sponges.

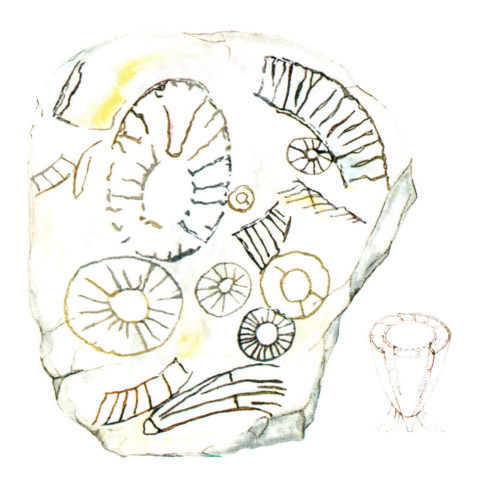

Archaeocyaths were marine organisms that contributed to the creation of the first reefs.

Sponges

Primary Features

Hydnoceras (**1**, Devonian-Carboniferous) is up to 30 cm tall, with criss-cross 'plaid' patterning. *Doryderma* (**2**, Carboniferous-Cretaceous) is tree-like with thick branches. *Plocoscyphia* (**3**, Cretaceous) is a complex network of tubes.

Stratigraphy and Distribution

Sponges are known from 1.5 billion years ago (Precambrian) to the present day.

Additional Information

The variously shaped sponges are usually told apart by the microscopic, calcareous or siliceous 'spicules' that make up the skeleton – almost always the only parts preserved.

Similar Forms

Corals, **archaeocyaths**.

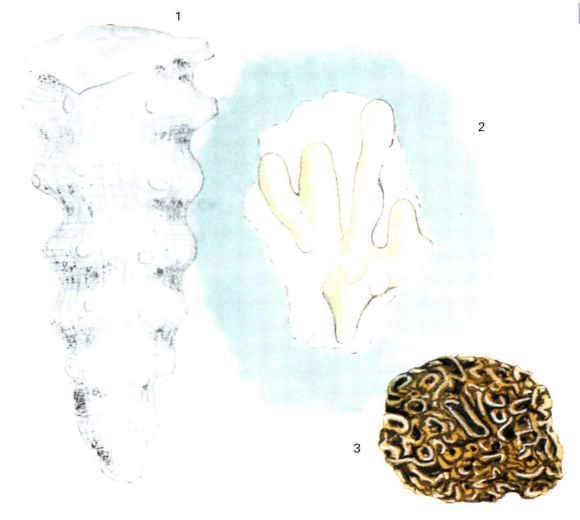

Rugose Corals

Primary Features

Hexagonaria (**1**, Devonian) and *Lonsdaleia* (**2**, Carboniferous) are superficially similar, massive forms with polygons left by the polyps, but differ in fine detail. Colonies of *Lithostrotion* (**3**, Carboniferous) are often bundles of tubes.

Stratigraphy and Distribution

Lower Ordovician to Permian marine rocks around the world.

Additional Information

Rugose corals are simple, solitary or colonial individuals, often horn-shaped with six prominent and up to four subsidiary vertical internal partitions, or septa.

Similar Forms

Scleractinian corals (only much older), archaeocyaths (only younger), sponges.

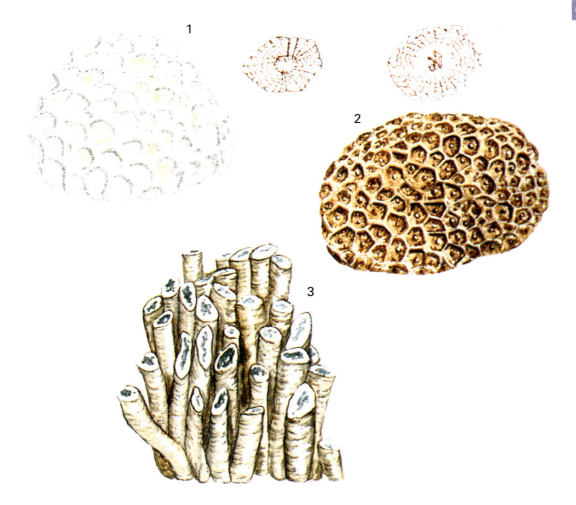

A colony of Lithostrotion fossils, a species of rugose coral.

Tabulate Corals

Primary Features

Favosites (**1**, Silurian-Devonian) is massive with tiny, boxlike spaces, but, *Coenites* (**2**, Silurian-Devonian) is often plant-like and branching. *Michelinia* (**3**, Carboniferous) has a honeycomb-like pattern.

Stratigraphy and Distribution

Lower Ordovician to Permian.

Additional Information

The colonial tabulate corals have prominent horizontal partitions (tabulae) and weaker septa.

Similar Forms

Other corals, sponges. Note that *Michelinia* lacks the septa prominent in rugose corals such as **Lonsdaleia** and **Hexagonaria**.

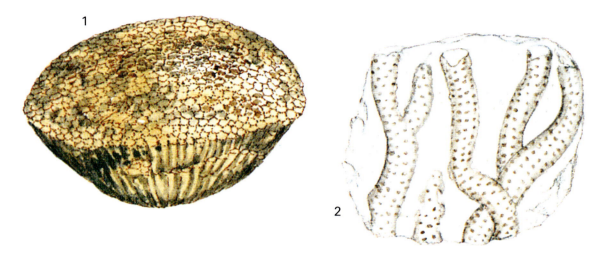

Favosites are tabulate corals which lived in shallow water, including reefs and calcareous shales.

Scleractinian Corals

Primary Features

Meandrina (**1**, Eocene-Recent) is a 'brain coral', while *Porites* (**2**, Eocene-Recent) may be branching, massive or encrusting, and has small, discontinuous septa. Both are found today.

Stratigraphy and Distribution

Scleractinian corals evolved in the mid-Triassic and are found in marine sediments around the world.

Additional Information

Solitary or colonial, scleractinian individuals have six septa, like **rugose corals**, but have six (as opposed to four) subsidiary septa.

Similar Forms

Other corals, sponges.

Scleractinian Corals

Primary Features

Cyclolites (**1**, Cretaceous-Eocene) is a solitary coral with many septa and a base (**2**) with concentric ridges. *Acropora* (**3**, Eocene-Recent) colonies have a delicate branched structure and are common today.

Stratigraphy and Distribution

Scleractinian corals evolved in the mid-Triassic and are found in marine sediments around the world.

Additional Information

Solitary or colonial, scleractinian individuals have six main septa like **rugose corals** but differ in having six (as opposed to four) subsidiary septa.

Similar Forms

Other corals, sponges.

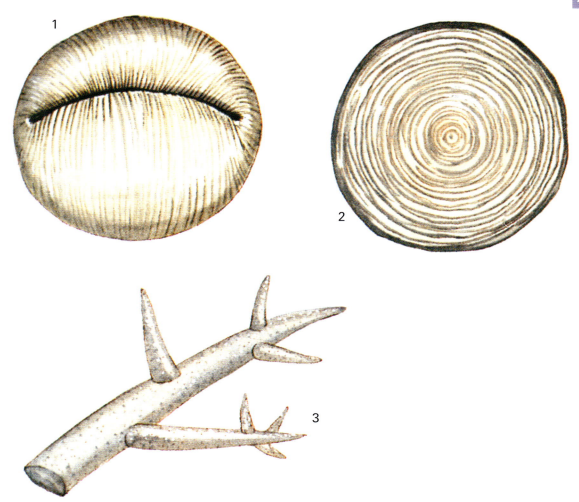

Bellerophon
Gastropods

Primary Features

Broad, symmetrical shell up to 8 cm across, with flared aperture such that smaller whorls are almost hidden by the larger ones. The deep notch or 'slit band' in the front margin of the aperture is a typical feature.

Stratigraphy and Distribution

Silurian to Triassic, worldwide.

Additional Information

Bellerophon was the first Palaeozoic mollusc to be described, in 1808. It is one of a group of about 70 Cambrian-Triassic molluscs distinguished by a slit band.

Similar Forms

Tremanotus (Ordovician-Silurian); *Boiotremus*, a planispiral shell with a wide aperture like a bugle.

Platyceras
Gastropods

Primary Features

A shell about 5 cm long in which the last whorl (nearest the aperture) is very large compared with the other, tightly curled whorls.

Stratigraphy and Distribution

Silurian-Permian, worldwide. A relatively common find in Devonian reef limestones.

Additional Information

The platyceratids included fast-growing, loosely coiled or conical shells found mainly in limestones of Ordovician-Permian age, sometimes associated with echinoderms.

Similar Forms

Mourlonia is similar to *Platyceras* but has a less extreme aperture.

The fossilized shell of the sea snail Platyceras has a distinctively large outside whorl.

Pleurotomaria
Gastropods

Primary Features

A broad shell up to 9 cm long, with a low, helical spire about 7 cm tall. The broad aperture has a slit near the upper edge, and the shell is heavily ornamented with bands of tubercles, grooves and growth lines.

Stratigraphy and Distribution

Lower Jurassic-Lower Cretaceous.

Additional Information

As with the unrelated *Bellerophon*, the 'slit band' results from the closure of the slit in the edge of the aperture with the growth of the successive whorls.

Similar Forms

None.

Pleurotomaria has a low, helical spire ornamented with bands of tubercles, grooves and growth lines.

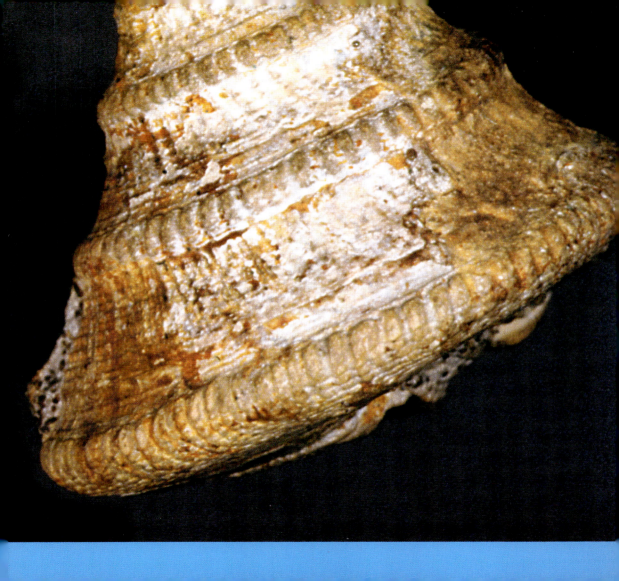

Natica
Gastropods

Primary Features

A smooth spherical to slightly conical shell up to 5 cm tall with large last whorl and a small spire. The aperture is semicircular with a thin outer lip and a thicker inner one contiguous with the rest of the shell.

Stratigraphy and Distribution

Triassic-Recent, worldwide.

Additional Information

The modern necklace shell is a carnivore, drilling circular holes in bivalves with the help of an acid secretion. These holes have been identified in Pliocene fossil bivalves.

Similar Forms

None.

Natica fed off bivalves by boring holes in their shell with acid to get to the animals inside.

Other Gastropods

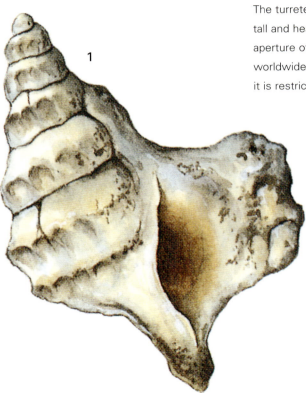

1

The turreted *Aporrhais* (1) is up to 12 cm tall and heavily sculptured with a flaring aperture often extended into 'fingers'. Found worldwide in the Jurassic and Cretaceous, it is restricted to the North Atlantic today.

Other Gastropods

2

Hippochrenes (2) has a conical spire up to 8 cm tall, equal in height to the width of the largest whorl. The upper lip of the aperture is fused to the spire and extended downwards into a tube. Eocene of Eurasia.

The gastropod Aporrhais often has a flaring aperture extended into 'fingers', as shown here.

Other Gastropods

1

Clavilithes (1) is up to 15 cm tall and has a robustly constructed spire with prominent shelf-like suture. The apex is sculpted but the rest of the shell is smooth. The aperture is extended downwards to form a long canal. Eocene-Pliocene, Northern Hemisphere.

Other Gastropods

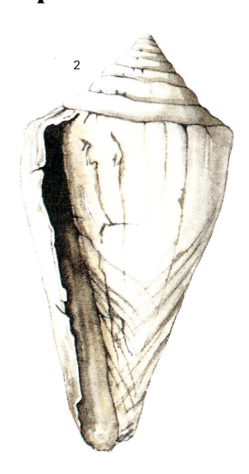

2

Conus (2) is a bioconical shell up to about 10 cm long with a very large last whorl and a slot-like aperture that is always longer than the height of all the upper whorls combined. A carnivore that kills its prey with powerful poisons, it is known from the Upper Cretaceous to the Recent and is a useful guide fossil in the Pliocene.

Conus used venom to kill their prey, which included polychaetes and some small fish.

Turritella
Gastropods

Primary Features

A tall, thin shell (**1**) about 5 cm high and with prominent ridges spiralling round the slightly convex whorls at right angles to the growth lines. The last whorl is similar to the others and ends abruptly with an oval aperture.

Stratigraphy and Distribution

Upper Cretaceous to Recent, worldwide. A useful guide fossil in the Eocene.

Additional Information

Several species are known today and are familiar sea-shore finds.

Similar Forms

The turreted shape has appeared several times in evolution. Examples include the gastropods *Cerithium* (**2**, Cretaceous-Recent, which unlike *Turritella* has a slot in the aperture for a siphon); *Loxonema* (Silurian) and *Microptychia* (Carboniferous), and the ammonite ***Turrilites*** (Cretaceous).

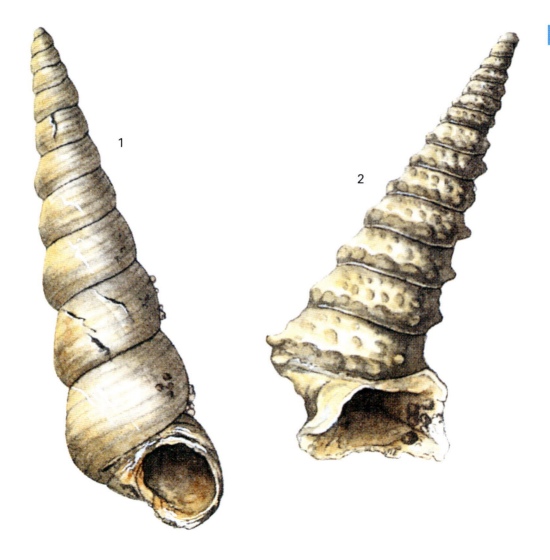

1

2

Turritella lived in the sediment of the sea floor where they filtered fine particles of food from the water, much as their descendants do today.

Planorbis

Gastropods

Primary Features

Small (less than 5 cm), smooth, deep-sutured, plane spirals flat on one side and concave on the other. There may be a low spire, and occasionally both faces are concave.

Stratigraphy and Distribution

Oligocene-Recent, Old World.

Additional Information

Although a freshwater mollusc, *Planorbis* is closely related to land snails and slugs.

Similar Forms

None.

Planorbis were freshwater molluscs whose shells coiled in flat planes.

The descendants of Nucula can be found on beaches today.

Arca

Bivalves

Primary Features

The convex shells are almost rectangular in shape with beaks displaced well towards the front and well separated from the toothed hinges. Decorated with radial ridges and a smaller number of widely spaced concentric lines.

Stratigraphy and Distribution

Jurassic-Recent, worldwide.

Additional Information

The Noah's Ark Shell *Arca noae* is a common Mediterranean and Atlantic species today, and grows up to 8 cm long.

Similar Forms

Parallelodon (up to 15 cm long, Devonian-Jurassic) has a shell of similar shape to that of *Arca* but smoother and with fewer teeth, confined to the front and back ends of the long hinge.

Glycymeris
Bivalves

Primary Features

Convex, circular, about 4–5 cm long with centrally placed, upward-pointing beaks. Radial ridges and fewer, more widely spaced concentric growth lines. The inside edge of the lower margin is decorated with small tubercles.

Stratigraphy and Distribution

Lower Cretaceous-Recent, worldwide. The Dog Cockle.

Additional Information

The hinges have teeth that tend to be more slanted with increasing distance from the beak on either side.

Similar Forms

None.

Glycycermis lived burrowed in gravel of up to 100m.

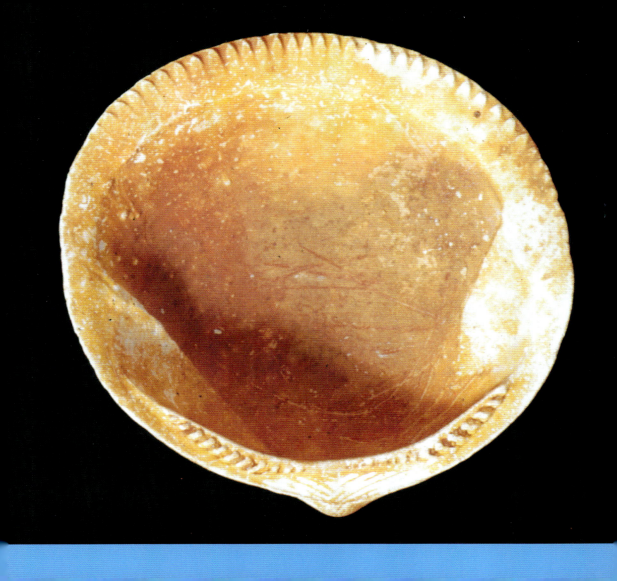

Pinna

Bivalves

Primary Features

An exaggeratedly fan-shaped and triangular shell up to 25 cm long. The smooth surface is punctuated with radial ridges near the pointed beak, undulating concentric ridges near the margin.

Stratigraphy and Distribution

Lower Carboniferous-Recent, worldwide.

Additional Information

The Fan Mussel.

Similar Forms

None; highly distinctive.

The Pinna was a large marine bivalve with a distinctive triangular shell.

Pecten

Bivalves

Primary Features

A familiar shell in which one quadrant-shaped valve is distinctly more convex than the other. The hinge is extended on either side by ear-like flanges. The shell is ornamented with broad ridges radiating from the beak.

Stratigraphy and Distribution

Upper Eocene-Recent.

Additional Information

The Scallop.

Similar Forms

Relatives of *Pecten* are known from the Triassic although similar shells are known from even older rocks, for example the Carboniferous form *Dunbarella*.

The Pecten is distinguished by its ear-like flanges and deep ridges.

Gryphaea

Bivalves

Primary Features

Up to about 15 cm long. The small, flat right valve contrasts with the large, convex left valve with its overhanging beak and with its ornamentation of strong concentric growth lines and lamellae. The hinge is toothless.

Stratigraphy and Distribution

Upper Triassic-Upper Jurassic. Limited to North America and Siberia in the Triassic but worldwide in the Lias. Common in Pliensbachian limestones but extinct by the Kimmeridgian.

Additional Information

The changing curvature of the 'Devil's Toenail' is a well-known example of evolutionary transformation.

Similar Forms

The ornamentation is similar to that of *Ostrea*.

The Gryphaea is also known as the 'Devil's Toenail'.

Ostrea

Bivalves

Primary Features

A variably shaped shell up to 20 cm across, with small, flat right valve and thick, convex left valve. The right valve is ornamented with growth lines, the left with a heavy sculpture of radial ridges and tubercles.

Stratigraphy and Distribution

Triassic to Recent, worldwide.

Additional Information

The common oyster.

Similar Forms

Convex left valve and flat right valve like *Gryphaea*, but less extreme.

The Ostrea fossil is the predecessor of today's common oyster.

Inoceramus

Bivalves

Primary Features

Shell usually between 5 and 15 cm tall and oval to rectangular in shape, with toothless upward-pointing beak and a long hinge line. The left valve is often more convex than the right.

Stratigraphy and Distribution

Lias to Upper Cretaceous.

Additional Information

The distinctive species of *Inoceramus* are useful zone fossils. Some species in the chalk may be more than 1 m long.

Similar Forms

Ornament in *Inoceramus* varies according to species; for example, *I. concentricus* (**1**) has strong concentric ripples, whereas *I. sulcatus* (**2**) – found in some deposits such as the English mid-Cretaceous – has sharply pointed radial ridges.

Some species of Inoceramus, such as this one, have concentric growth lines, whereas others have radial ridges.

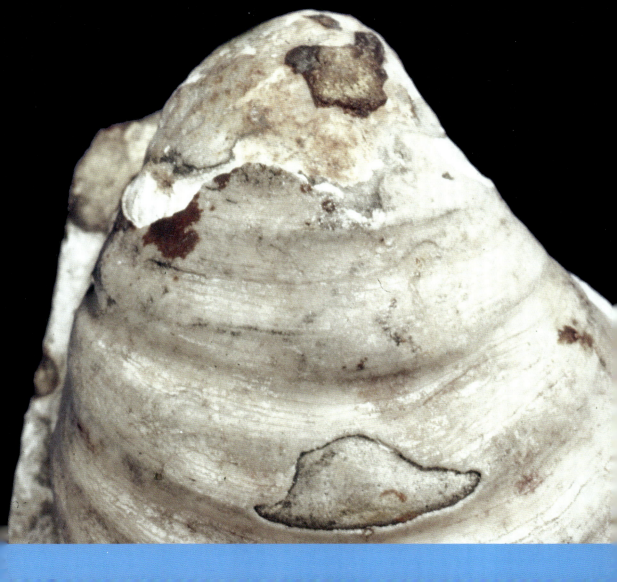

Spondylus
Bivalves

Primary Features

Taller (up to 12 cm) than broad, oval in outline, the spiny shell surface looks like a chair after an attack by a family of kittens. It has an ornament of radial ridges of varying strength, spacing and pattern.

Stratigraphy and Distribution

Lower Jurassic-Recent, worldwide.

Additional Information

The Thorny Oyster *S. gaederopus.*

Similar Forms

None.

Trigonia
Bivalves

Primary Features

A thick, often pearly, triangular shell about 5 cm long, decorated with concentric, sausage-like ridges on the front half of each valve, weaker radial ridges on the back half, the halves separated by a prominent keel. The hinge has five teeth.

Stratigraphy and Distribution

Middle Triassic to Upper Cretaceous, worldwide.

Additional Information

Once common, the only surviving relative is the Australasian *Neotrigonia*.

Similar Forms

Unmistakeable.

Trigonia can be identified by the strong ridges on the front half of each valve.

Mya
Bivalves

Primary Features

A long, narrow, oval to rectangular shell between 3–15 cm broad with rather flat valves and a small beak. The smooth surface may have faint concentric growth lines.

Stratigraphy and Distribution

Oligocene to Recent.

Additional Information

The gaper shells. A spoon-shaped process or chondrophore replaces teeth inside the hinge.

Similar Forms

Gervillella (Triassic-Cretaceous, up to 25 cm) resembles *Mya* but is even longer and narrower, and is ornamented with strong concentric growth lines and has a hinge armed with long, slender teeth.

Mya lived buried in tidal mudflats.

Nautilus
Cephalopods

Primary Features

A smooth shell 15–25 cm in diameter with simple suture lines. It is involute, in that the younger, outer chambers obscure the smaller, inner ones.

Stratigraphy and Distribution

Oligocene to Recent.

Additional Information

Found nowadays in Australasian waters, the nautilus is the only modern cephalopod with an external shell, with the possible exception of females of the unrelated 'paper nautilus' *Argonauta*.

Similar Forms

Several rather similar species are known throughout geological time,

for example *Aturia* (Palaeocene-Miocene, worldwide).

The suture lines of the Nautilus delineate chambers within the shell.

Palaeozoic Nautiloids

Cephalopods

Lituites (**1**) is about 12 cm long. The shell is straight except for the end, which is coiled tightly. Middle Ordovician of Northern Europe, especially Sweden.

Palaeozoic Nautiloids

Cephalopods

Dawsonoceras (2) from the Silurian is found as corrugated rods about 3 cm in diameter. Its relatives survived to the Triassic; the siphuncle running down the middle of the straight shells passed through a simple collar at the junction of each septum.

Bactrites (3) had a long, slender shell and, unusually, a siphuncle running along one edge rather than down the middle. The smallest chamber or 'protoconch' is bulbous, the whole shell looking like a sherry trumpet. The sutures were simple but with a ventral lobe. Upper Silurian to Permian of Central Europe, Sicily and Russia.

3

Early Ammonoids
Cephalopods

Goniatites (1) is about 4–5 cm across, and comes from the Lower Carboniferous of England, Germany, Belgium and North Africa. The shell is thick, smooth and involute. Suture lines have smooth, lateral but zigzagged ventral lobes. Similar forms include *Tornoceras* (Middle Devonian), *Manticoceras* (Upper Devonian), *Homoceras* and *Reticuloceras* (Carboniferous).

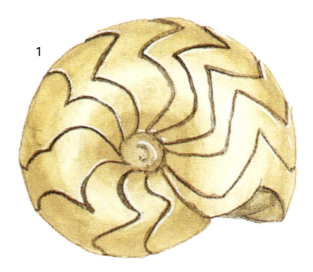

1

Early Ammonoids
Cephalopods

Gastrioceras (2) from the Upper Carboniferous (Coal Measures) is 3–4 cm across and is found worldwide. It is evolute (all whorls showing) and decorated with heavy ridges that branch and lighten towards the venter (bottom edge). The suture has curved lobes and pointed saddles.

2

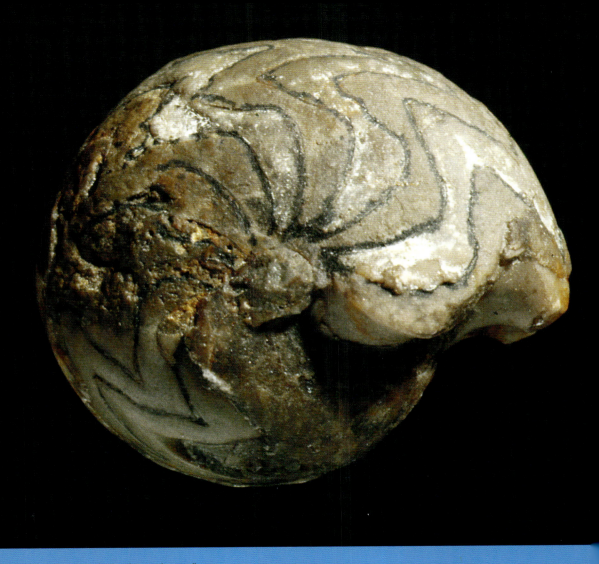

The Goniatite has distinctive zigzagged suture lines.

Ceratites

Cephalopods

Primary Features

An ammonoid about 5–10 cm across with a smooth convolute shell (midway between evolute and involute). The suture has simple saddles but serrated lobes.

Stratigraphy and Distribution

Lower Triassic ('Muschelkalk') of Europe.

Additional Information

Ceratitids were widespread in the Triassic but became extinct before the end of the period.

Similar Forms

Similar forms include *Cenoceras* (a nautiloid, rather than an ammonoid) and *Trachyceras* (Mid- to Upper Triassic).

Wavy suture lines can help distinguish a Ceratite.

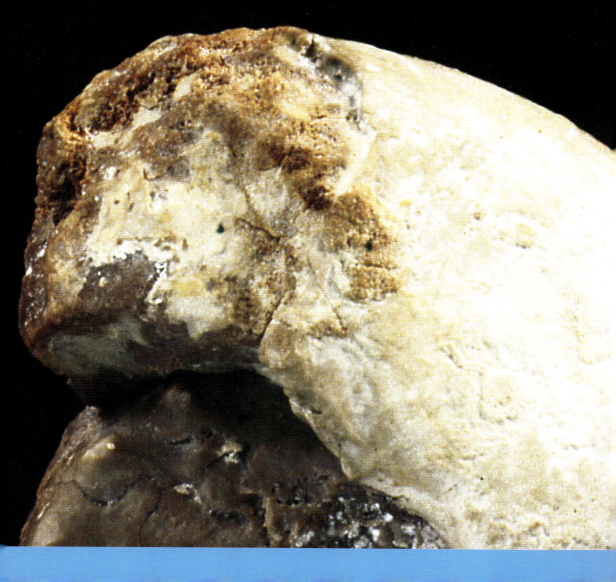

Arnioceras

Cephalopods

Primary Features

An ammonite about 5–6 cm across, evolute and flattened with a wide umbilicus, whorls squarish in section with a strong keel and ribs that curve forwards as they run towards the venter.

Stratigraphy and Distribution

Early Lower Jurassic (Sinemurian), worldwide.

Additional Information

An excellent zone fossil for the Sinemurian.

Similar Forms

Similar forms include the Sinemurian *Asteroceras* and *Echioceras* and the Pliensbachian *Uptonia*.

Arnioceras come from the Early Lower Jurassic period and are found worldwide.

Lower Jurassic Ammonites

Cephalopods

Asteroceras (**1**) is a stoutly built ammonite about 10 cm across, with a broad umbilicus and squarish whorls like **Arnioceras** but which increase in size more rapidly towards the aperture. The lateral face bears prominent ribs and there is a strong keel with furrows on each side. The sutures are complex with pointed lobes and broad, zigzagged saddles. Sinemurian, Northern Hemisphere.

Dactylioceras (**2**) is about 5–10 cm across, flat with a wide umbilicus and whorls circular in section. The strong ribs fork and flatten towards the venter but meet across it, so there is no keel. Lookalikes include the Upper Bajocian *Parkinsonia* (note the narrow groove along venter) and the Toarcian *Hildoceras.*

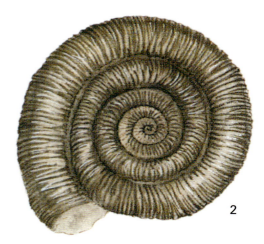

2

1

Lower Jurassic Ammonites

Cephalopods

Hildoceras (**3**) is an evolute shell up to 20 cm across with whorls of rectangular section that increase in size rapidly towards the aperture. Strong, arching ribs on surfaces facing away from the umbilicus, and tubercles near the seam. The keel is strong with furrows on either side. The suture has broad lobes and serrated saddles. Toarcian, Old World.

3

The serpentine Dactylioceras were sometimes referred to as 'snakestones' in ancient folklore.

Phylloceras
Cephalopods

Primary Features

A flattened, discus-shaped, involute ammonite 10–15 cm across, with a small umbilicus and a highly complex suture pattern of pointed lobes and characteristically leaflike saddles. The surface is smooth or finely lined.

Stratigraphy and Distribution

Lower Jurassic to Upper Cretaceous, worldwide.

Additional Information

The persistence of *Phylloceras* in the geological column is notable among the usually short-lived ammonites.

Similar Forms

Similar forms include *Harpoceras* (Toarcian), *Tragophylloceras* (Pliensbachian) and *Leioceras* (Aalenian).

The unusual and complex suture lines of the Phylloceras are described as 'ammonitic'.

Middle Jurassic Ammonites

Cephalopods

Perisphinctes (1) is a large, evolute ammonite (30 cm across, occasionally much larger) which has deep square-section whorls with ribs that fork toward the venter. The sutures are highly complex. Middle-Upper Jurassic, Old World.

1

Middle Jurassic Ammonites

Cephalopods

Macrocephalites (2) from the Lower Callovian of Europe is about 10 cm across, thick, involute and decorated with many closely spaced ribs that meet across the venter. Similar forms include *Leioceras* (Aalenian) and *Clydoniceras* (Bathonian). Lower Callovian, Europe.

2

Hoplites
Cephalopods

Primary Features

A convolute form about 5–10 cm across, with a deep but rather narrow umbilicus and the venter sunk into a crease. Ribs radiating from tubercles on the shoulder fork forwards towards the venter.

Stratigraphy and Distribution

Albian of Europe and Asia.

Additional Information

Hoplites is a distinctive zone fossil for the Lower part of the Albian stage.

Similar Forms

Similar to the Middle-Upper Albian *Euhoplites*.

The Hoplites has strong ribbing radiating from the shoulder into the venter.

Cretaceous Ammonites

Cephalopods

Mortoniceras (1) is flattened, evolute and about 15–25 cm across, with a strong fur-owed keel. Ribs originating from tubercles near shoulder and on the lateral surface run towards the venter. Albian, worldwide.

1

Cretaceous Ammonites

Cephalopods

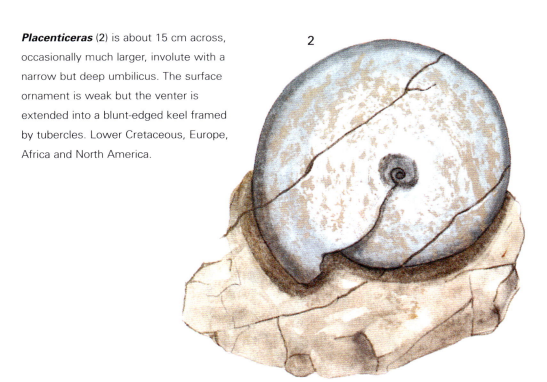

Placenticeras (2) is about 15 cm across, occasionally much larger, involute with a narrow but deep umbilicus. The surface ornament is weak but the venter is extended into a blunt-edged keel framed by tubercles. Lower Cretaceous, Europe, Africa and North America.

2

Unusual Cretaceous Ammonites

Cephalopods

Scaphites (1) is an involute ammonite about 10 cm across, ornamented with many fine, branching ribs. The shell is progressively more loosely coiled towards the aperture. Cenomanian, worldwide.

Crioceras (2) has a loose, open, ramshorn-shape. Hauterivian, worldwide.

Hamites (3) is a loose, open coil broadening into a shape like a curtain hook. The sutures are very complex. Albian, worldwide.

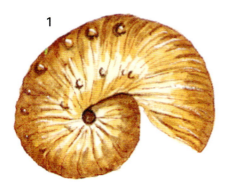

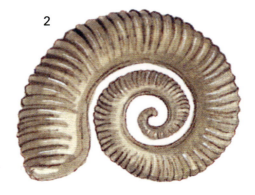

Unusual Cretaceous Ammonites

Cephalopods

Turrilites (4) forms a helical spiral like the gastropod *Turritella* except that it has suture lines and an open seam between the whorls. It is also much larger, sometimes more than 30 cm tall. Cretaceous, worldwide.

Baculites (5) is a long, straight form more than 10 cm long, with complex sutures but no other ornament. It looks very like a nautiloid except that the shell is flat in section. Cretaceous, worldwide.

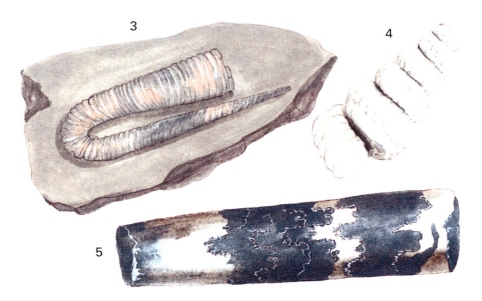

3

4

5

Hamites are unusual ammonites because they are hook-shaped as opposed to curled into a coil.

Belemnitella

Belemnites

Primary Features

A large belemnite (**1**) about 10 cm long, circular in section but with a flattened ridge running along the top surface, with grooves on either side.

Stratigraphy and Distribution

Cretaceous of Europe.

Additional Information

The bullet-shaped belemnites (Carboniferous-Eocene) are common fossils in Jurassic and Cretaceous rocks. They are the resistant internal skeletons of squid-like animals.

Similar Forms

Other common belemnites include *Cylindroteuthis* (**2**) (Jurassic-Cretaceous of Europe and North America), *Belemnopsis* (**3**) (Lower Jurassic of Eurasia) and *Neohibolites* (Upper Cretaceous of Europe).

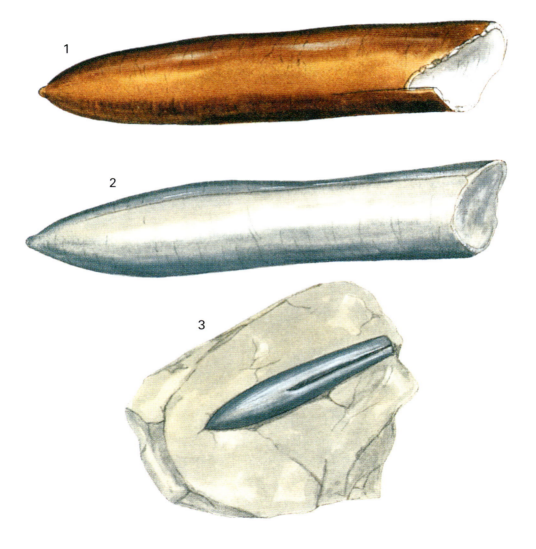

Agnostid Trilobites

Trilobites

Triplagnostus (**1**) is a small (less than 1 cm long), eyeless form in which the head and tail are the same size and shape. The glabella is divided into triangular front and elongate hind lobes, and there are no facial sutures. The genal angle may bear a small spine. Thorax only 2 segments, tail looks very similar to head. Similar forms include *Agnostus* (Upper Cambrian), *Condylopyge* (Middle Cambrian) and **Eodiscus** (Lower-Middle Cambrian).

1

Agnostid Trilobites
Trilobites

Eodiscus (2), at less than 5 mm long, is even smaller than *Triplagnostus*. The head and tail are the same size (and often found separately). The glabella has neither eyes nor facial sutures and is convex with a sharp, occasionally spiny, genal angle. The thorax has 2–3 segments. The tail axis is pronounced, with strong transverse grooves. Lower-Middle Cambrian.

2

Olenellus
Trilobites

Primary Features

A spiny form about 3 cm long, with a broad, semicircular head larger than the tail. The eyes are prominent and crescent-shaped. The border in front of the bulbous glabella extends into sharp genal spines. Thorax has 9 segments, tail about 6.

Stratigraphy and Distribution

Lower Cambrian of Scotland and North America.

Additional Information

Olenellus is one of the earliest known trilobites and an important indicator ('zone fossil') for Lower Cambrian rocks, especially in Scotland and N. America.

Similar Forms

Callavia is similar but lacks the long tail-spine and occurs in Scandinavia and in the West Midlands of England.

Olenellus is one of the earliest known trilobites.

Paradoxides

Trilobites

Primary Features

Small (2 cm) to large, the head is much bigger than the tail, which may be obscured by thoracic spines. Eyes and glabella prominent, genal spines extend backwards about half the length of the body. Thorax has between 13 and 22 segments.

Stratigraphy and Distribution

Important zone fossil for Middle Cambrian (St David's) rocks in Europe, North Africa and North America.

Additional Information

Among the largest trilobites; specimens from Bohemia may be more than 50 cm long.

Similar Forms

Similar forms include *Hydrocephalus*.

The Paradoxides seen here is from Bohemia and approaches 1 m in length.

Cryptolithus
Trilobites

Primary Features

About 1 cm long, the head is the same size as the rest of the body combined. The glabella is narrow but very convex and widens forwards. The wide, ornamented front border extends into long genal spines that may extend behind the body.

Stratigraphy and Distribution

Lower-Middle Ordovician of England and North America.

Additional Information

The similar *Trinucleus* has a deeply furrowed glabella and is an important Ordovician zone fossil in Britain and Scandinavia.

Similar Forms

Other similar forms from the Ordovician include *Stapeleyella*, *Omnia* and *Tretaspis*.

The head of the Cryptolithus is the same size as the rest of its body.

Bumastus
Trilobites

Primary Features

A large (5 cm), smooth form in which the head and tail are the same size. The glabella, axis and genal angles are ill-defined and the fossil looks like nothing more than a giant woodlouse. The thorax has 8–10 segments.

Stratigraphy and Distribution

Ordovician and Silurian of Europe.

Additional Information

Particularly well known from the Ordovician of Bohemia and the Silurian Wenlock limestones of England.

Similar Forms

The Ordovician *Illaenus* is similar but the trilobation is not quite as well-effaced as in *Bumastus*.

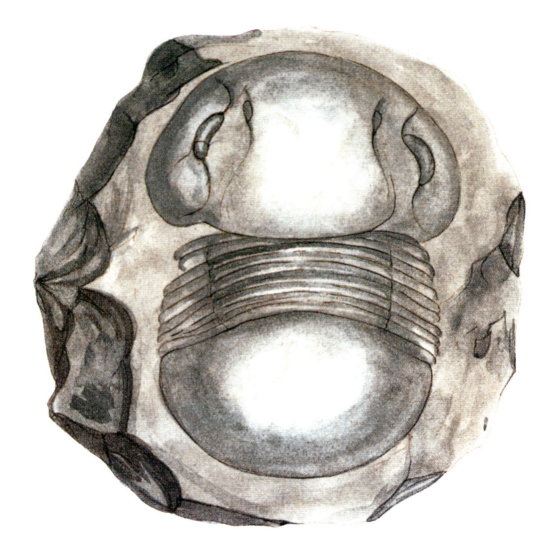

Phacops
Trilobites

Primary Features

Between 3 and 8 cm long, the head is much larger than the tail and has a big, ornamented glabella that broadens forward. Eyes big and kidney-shaped, genal angles smooth and blunt. The thorax has about 11 segments.

Stratigraphy and Distribution

Silurian and Devonian, worldwide. An important zone fossil in the Devonian.

Additional Information

Often found curled up into a ball like a modern woodlouse.

Similar Forms

Similar forms include the Silurian *Acaste* and **Calymene**.

Phacops can be recognized from their large eyes and ornamented glabella.

Calymene
Trilobites

Primary Features

5–8 cm long, the rounded tail is much smaller than the semicircular head. The glabella is swollen into 3 pairs of lobes, with a deep groove dividing it from the front edge. The eyes are large and the genal angle smooth.

Stratigraphy and Distribution

Lower Silurian-Middle Devonian.

Additional Information

Calymene blumenbachi is well known from Silurian (Wenlock) limestone although related species occur widely in Europe, the Americas and Australia.

Similar Forms

Similar forms include **Phacops** as well as the Silurian *Acaste* and *Cheirurus*.

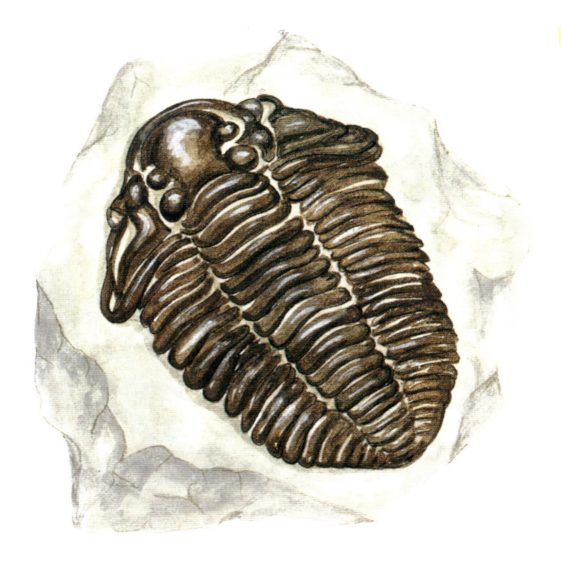

Many Calymene are found like this; rolled into a ball in order to defend themselves and to protect their soft, vulnerable undersides.

Dalmanites

Trilobites

Primary Features

About 4 cm long, the large glabella widens forwards and is cut with small transverse furrows. The thorax has 10–12 segments: the tail is the same size as the head with a smooth trailing edge extended into a long spine.

Stratigraphy and Distribution

Dalmanites proeva is an important Middle Ordovician zone fossil in Europe. Other species in the genus occur in Europe, the Americas and Australia.

Additional Information

The lenses in the large kidney-shaped compound eyes of *Dalmanites* are often large enough to be individually visible to the naked eye or magnifying glass.

Similar Forms

The Devonian *Odontochile* is similar.

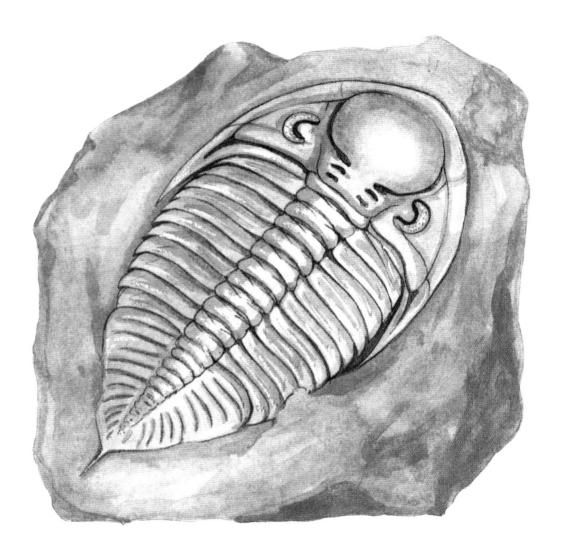

The Dalmanites has large kidney-shaped eyes. Trilobites developed the earliest and most advanced visual systems.

Eurypterus
Eurypterids

Primary Features

A scorpion-like animal about 10–30 cm long with six pairs of legs, the last pair developed as large swimming paddles. The abdomen terminates in a long spine.

Stratigraphy and Distribution

Ordovician-Carboniferous, Eurasia and North America. *E. fischeri* is common in the Scandinavian Silurian.

Additional Information

Eurypterids were marine predators, related to the modern scorpion.

Similar Forms

A length of up to 3 m makes *Pterygotus* the largest arthropod of all time. The tail ended in a broad, flat 'fluke' and unlike *Eurypterus* it has a pair of long-stemmed pincers, each one up to 20 cm long.

The Eurypterus is related to the modern scorpion.

Balanus
Crustaceans

Primary Features

Barnacles are sedentary crustaceans living in conical shells made of 4–6 calcified plates. An aperture in the apex of the cone, protected by valves, allows the animal to wave its limbs in the water to breathe and catch prey.

Stratigraphy and Distribution

Eocene-Recent, worldwide.

Additional Information

Barnacles are common everywhere today, particularly in the intertidal zone where they attach themselves to solid surfaces, occasionally in great numbers.

Similar Forms

None.

Insects in Amber

Amber is the hardened resin of coniferous trees. Generally rare although locally abundant (for example in the Oligocene of the Baltic), it may contain the remains of insects that became trapped in the sticky resin before it solidified. Insects evolved in the Devonian and are the most abundant animals today, although their physical delicacy makes for a rather patchy fossil record.

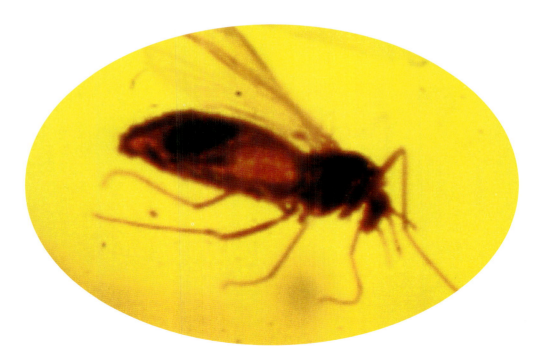

Amber is fossilized tree sap. Most of the world's amber is in the region of 30–90 million years old.

Pseudohornera

Trepostome Bryozoans

Primary Features

Delicate, mould-like branching networks (**1**) of thin tubes growing across rock planes.

Stratigraphy and Distribution

Mainly Ordovician marine limestones, especially in Europe and North America. Trepostomes became much rarer after the Ordovician and probably died out in the Permian or Triassic.

Additional Information

Trepostome colonies are made of long, thin tubes joined either in a branching fashion (as here) or as massive encrustations.

Similar Forms

Massive, coral-like forms such as *Monticulipora* (**2**). Some branching trepostomes such as *Constellaria* (**3**) have distinctive star-shaped patterns on their surfaces.

Cryptostome Bryozoans

Primary Featurs

The spiral-like axis of *Archimedes* (**1**, Carboniferous-Permian) is the most easily identified bryozoan. It is sometimes found bearing lace-like sheets indistinguishable from *Fenestella* (**2**, Devonian), or *Polypora* (**3**, Ordovician-Permian).

Stratigraphy and Distribution

Marine limestone or Ordovician to Permian age.

Additional Information

Cryptostome colonies grew erect (as in *Archimedes*), or in flat encrusting sheets.

Similar Forms

Other bryozoans, sponges and corals.

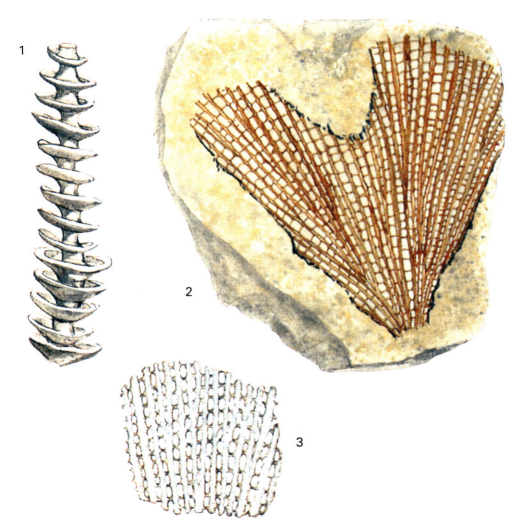

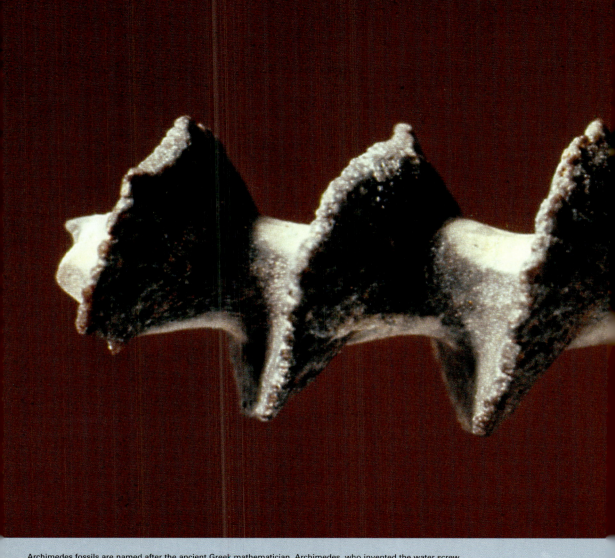

Archimedes fossils are named after the ancient Greek mathematician, Archimedes, who invented the water screw.

Cyclostome and Cheilostome Bryozoans

Primary Features

The branching cyclostome *Meliceritites* (**1**, Cretaceous) contrasts with the small (1 cm) circular cheilostome *Lunulites* (**2**, Cretaceous-Eocene), with its flattened or slightly conical colonies.

Stratigraphy and Distribution

Cyclostomes (Ordovician-Recent) and cheilostomes (Jurassic-Recent) include modern bryozoa. The fossils are found in marine limestones, particularly in Europe and North America

Additional Information

Cyclostomes are made of simple calcareous tubes fused together to form colonies of variable shape. Cheilostomes are even more variable, with delicate, sheet-like and encrusting forms.

Similar Forms

Encrusting cyclostomes like *Alveolaria* (Oligocene-Pliocene) and cheilostomes like *Onychocella* (Cretaceous-Recent) look very like 'brain' corals; others resemble plant stems. Examination by microscope is often the only way to find the features needed to identify bryozoa exactly.

1

2

Lunulites are Cheilostome Bryozoans.

Lingula
Inarticulate Brachiopods

Primary Features

Translucent, horny, spoon-shaped shells almost equal in size, tapering towards the back.

Stratigraphy and Distribution

Silurian to Recent. Found in shales often without other brachiopod species.

Additional Information

The modern form, found off the coasts of Japan, has changed little since the genus first appeared.

Similar Forms

The valves of *Lingulella* (Cambrian to Middle Ordovician) are similar to those of *Lingula* but smaller (2 cm long) and taper more gently towards the back. The pedicle valve has a groove for the pedicle.

The Lingula has not changed much in 400 million years.

Inarticulate Brachiopods

Obolella shells (**1**) are ovoid, calcareous and biconvex, and are typical of a few similar genera of inarticulate brachiopods confined to the Lower and Middle Cambrian.

Orbiculoidea shells (**2**) are small and circular with concentric rings. The brachial valve is conical, but the pedicle valve is flat with a slot for the pedicle running from the centre to the back edge. Ordovician to Permian.

1

2

Inarticulate Brachiopods

Crania shells (3) are calcareous, ovoid and about 1 cm long. The conical brachial valve lacks a pedicle and anchors directly to the substrate, which may be another brachiopod. Cretaceous-Recent.

3

Orthis
Articulate Brachiopods

Primary Features

Slightly biconvex, semicircular shell with radial ridges, 1–2 cm along the straight hinge, narrow interarea but open delthyrium. The hinge is not the widest part of the shell.

Stratigraphy and Distribution

Cambrian to Ordovician, worldwide.

Additional Information

Orthids (Lower Cambrian-Upper Permian) are rounded, biconvex to plano-convex shells, strophic with open delthyria. Simple brachidium comprising a pair of crura.

Similar Forms

Dalmanella (Ordovician-Silurian, worldwide) is circular, about 3 cm across, with fine, variably spaced radial ridges and concentric ridges near the front edge. *Jivinella* from the Bohemian Lower Ordovician has a pedicle valve with a pronounced apex and coarse radial ribbing.

Orthis fossils appeared in the Early Cambrian period then became very diverse in the Ordovician.

Leptaena
Articulate Brachiopods

Primary Features

A nearly rectangular shell with a long hinge line across the widest part of the shell (about 2 cm). The pedicle valve is sharply convex, the brachial valve concave. Decorated with radial ribs and wavy, concentric corrugations.

Stratigraphy and Distribution

Middle Ordovician to Devonian, worldwide; a common form in the Silurian.

Additional Information

A member of the strophomenids (Lower Ordovician to Lower Jurassic) which, with about 400 genera, is the largest and most diverse brachiopod group.

Similar Forms

None.

The Leptaena is nearly rectangular with a long hinge line across the widest part of the shell.

Other Strophomenids

Articulate Brachiopods

Strophomena (1) is a semicircular, biconvex shell in which a fold in the brachial valve is matched by a groove in the pedicle valve. Middle-Upper Ordovician.

1

Other Strophomenids
Articulate Brachiopods

Sowerbyella (2) is a small shell (1 cm across), with a concave brachial and convex pedicle valve, ornamented with fine radiating grooves. Ordovician to Lower Silurian, worldwide. Similar forms include *Aegiromena* (Middle Ordovician shales worldwide) and the large, winged shells of *Cymostrophia* from Devonian reef limestones in Europe and North America.

2

Sowerbyella is a common strophomenid brachiopod.

Other Strophomenids

Articulate Brachiopods

Productus (1) a semicircular shell about 3 cm across with the hinge line across the widest part. The beak of the strongly convex pedicle valve overhangs the hinge line, but the brachial valve is flat or concave. Decorated with close-set radial ridges, concentric corrugations and the bases of spines. Carboniferous, Eurasia.

1

Other Strophomenids

Articulate Brachiopods

Chonetes (2) a semicircular, strophic shell with four long spines protruding from the hinge line. Silurian, Europe.

2

The Productus is a semicircular shell decorated with close-set radial ridges and concentric corrugations.

Pentamerus

Articulate Brachiopods

Primary Features

A smooth, oval, highly biconvex shell about 4 cm long, with strongly incurved beaks overhanging a short, curved hinge line. Wide delthyrium but no interareas.

Stratigraphy and Distribution

A common Silurian form worldwide.

Additional Information

Pentamerids (Middle Cambrian-Upper Devonian) were often highly convex with curved beaks as in *Pentamerus*, and are common in Silurian and Devorian marine shelly limestones.

Similar Forms

Other pentamerids such as *Conchidium* and *Sieberella*.

Other Pentamerids

Articulate Brachiopods

Conchidium (**1**) is similar to *Pentamerus* but even more biconvex and has prominent radial ribs. With shells up to 10 cm long, it is among the largest pentamerids. Silurian-Lower Devonian, often found with fossil corals in limestones of Bohemia, England and North America.

1

Other Pentamerids

Articulate Brachiopods

Sieberella (2) is up to 5 cm long with a pedicle valve even more convex than in *Conchidium* or *Pentamerus*. The shell is smooth except for ridges that ornament a fold on the brachial valve that matches a ridged groove in the pedicle valve. Silurian-Devonian, worldwide. Similar forms include *Ivdelinia* (Lower Devonian, Europe) and *Gypidula* (Silurian-Lower Devonian), like *Sieberella* but rather smaller.

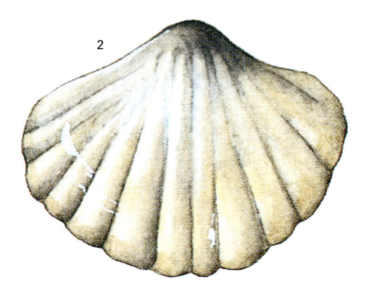

2

Rhynchonella
Articulate Brachiopods

Primary Features

Smooth, triangular shells about 2 cm long. The beak on the pedicle valve is sharp and projects above the pedicle foramen and the short, curved hinge line. A groove in the pedicle valve matches a deep fold in the brachial valve.

Stratigraphy and Distribution

Characteristic of the European Middle Jurassic.

Additional Information

Rhynchonellids had their heyday in the Mosozoic, although they are known from the Ordovician to the present day. Shells are often ribbed to give a zigzag outline to the front edge.

Similar Forms

Similar forms include the spherical *Sphaerirhynchia* (Middle Silurian-Devonian), *Trigonorhynchia* (Silurian) *Hypothyridina* (Devonian), *Pleuropugnoides* (Carboniferous), *Tetrarhynchia* (Jurassic) and *Cyclothyris* (Cretaceous).

Rhynchonella lived on the sea-bed in warm, shallow waters.

Spirifer

Articulate Brachiopods

Primary Features

A 'winged' shell up to 7 cm along the hinge. The pedicle valve beak is prominent with a larger interarea than on the brachial valve. A deep groove in the pedicle valve is matched by a fold in the brachial valve.

Stratigraphy and Distribution

Devonian-Permian, worldwide; a useful zone fossil in the Carboniferous.

Additional Information

Spiriferids are known from the Middle Ordovician to the Jurassic. Their shape is variable but they tend to have a spiral-shaped brachidium and a long hinge line.

Similar Forms

Similar forms include *Eospirifer* (Lower Devonian, Eurasia), *Cyrtospirifer* (Upper Devonian-Lower Carboniferous), *Mucrospirifer* and *Paraspirifer* (useful zone fossils in the Devonian).

Spirifer have wide hinges, up to 7cm long.

Other Spiriferids

Articulate Brachiopods

Atrypa (1) is longer (up to 4 cm) than broad, with a convex brachial valve and a flat cr slightly convex pedicle valve, in which there is a groove to accommodate a fold on the brachial valve. The ornament is a spiny meshwork of radial ridges crossed by concentric lines. Silurian-Devonian.

1

Other Spiriferids

Articulate Brachiopods

Cyrtia (2) is smooth and circular with a deep, convex pedicle valve with a very large interarea. A fold on the brachial valve fits into a groove in the pedicle valve. Silurian-Devonian, worldwide.

2

Atrypa survived nearly 100 million years from the Silurian to the Devonian.

Terebratulina

Articulate Brachiopods

Primary Features

An oval, biconvex shell that tapers towards the beak. The hinge line is short and gently curved. Fine ribs radiate from the beak. The hole for the pedicle is large, and the delthyrium closed by small plates.

Stratigraphy and Distribution

Jurassic-Recent, but a useful zone fossil in the Miocene and Pliocene.

Additional Information

Terebratulids are known from the Silurian to the present day, although they were at their peak in the Mesozoic. Their most characteristic feature is the large pedicle foramen.

Similar Forms

Gryphus and *Argyrotheca* still live in the Mediterranean, whereas *Magellania* inhabits the Pacific.

Other Terebratulids

Articulate Brachiopods

Terebratula (1) is up to 10 cm long, smooth, biconvex and similar to *Terebratulina*. The front edge is gently crinkled, and the hinge line is curved. The pedicle foramen is large and bordered by delthyrial plates. Miocene-Pliocene.

Pygites (2) is a distinctive shell with a central hole caused by rapid and unequal growth rates in the shell. Jurassic. The related *Pygope* is a Jurassic-Cretaceous zone fossil and well known from Italian marble quarries.

1

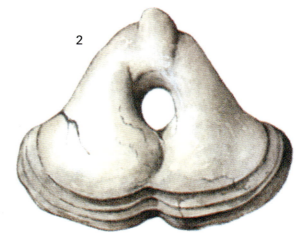

2

Other Terebratulids

Articulate Brachiopods

Sellithyris (3) is a smooth shell with a flattened, biconvex shape and a crinkled anterior edge. Cretaceous, Europe.

Stringocephalus (4) spheroid shell up to 10 cm across with the brachial valve more convex than the pedicle valve, which has a prominent hooked beak and pedicle foramen. Middle Devonian of Europe, and locally very abundant in shallow-water marine limestones.

3

4

The Terebratula is relatively smooth but with visible growth lines.

Edrioaster

Edrioasteroids

Primary Features

Ball-shaped body (**1**) about 2 cm across wrapped with five sinuous double-rowed food grooves (four with anticlockwise twists, the other with a clockwise twist) alternating with areas of irregular plates.

Stratigraphy and Distribution

Middle Ordovician of Europe and North America.

Additional Information

Edrioasteroids were a small group that appeared in the Lower Cambrian and died out in the Lower Carboniferous. Most known species come from Europe and North America.

Similar Forms

Coin-sized, pentagonal *Stromatocystites* (**2**) from the Lower-Middle Cambrian of Europe has five straight, narrow food grooves and is one of the earliest known of all echinoderms.

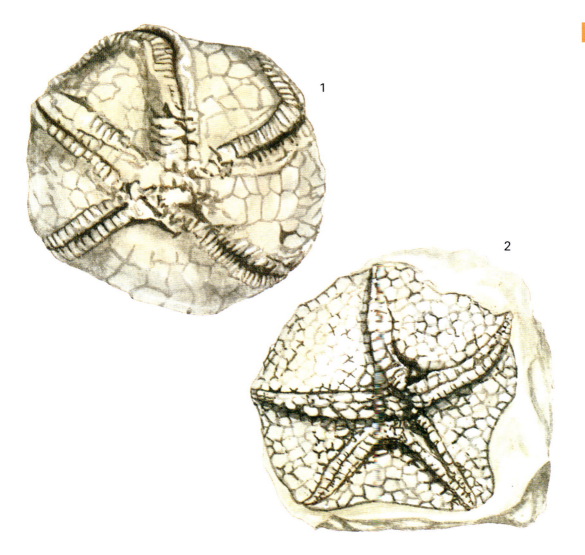

1

2

Cystoids

Echinosphaerites (1) is a flask-shaped diploporite cystoid, clothed in hexagonal plates.
The triangular mouth is bordered by three knobby joints for the arms. Ordovician, Sweden
and Bohemia. Similar forms include *Haplosphaeronis* and *Aristocystites*. Cystoids are found
in marine sediments of Cambrian-Devonian age.

1

Cystoids

Cheirocrinus (**2**) is a rhombiferan cystoid with a regular goblet-shaped theca, a stalk and several short tentacles. Ordovician of England. Similar forms include the Silurian *Pseudocrinites* and *Lepocrinites*.

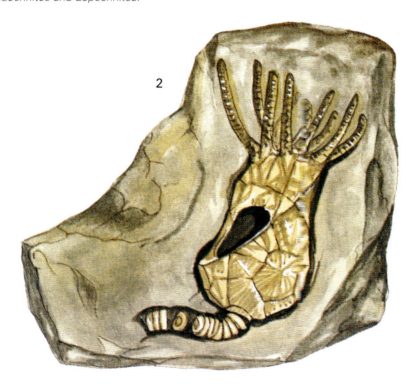

2

Orbitremites

Blastoids

Primary Features

Rugby-ball-shaped body, 1–2 cm tall, with five prominent food grooves. Body has 13 plates arranged in three rings: three basals, five radials and five triangular upper plates between the food grooves.

Stratigraphy and Distribution

Locally abundant in the Upper Carboniferous of Northern England.

Additional Information

80 genera of blastoid are known. Restricted to North America in the Silurian, they had spread worldwide by the Devonian but became extinct around the end of the Carboniferous.

Similar Forms

The slightly larger and more angular *Orophocrinus* can be found in the same rocks as *Orbitremites*.

70 species are included in the North American genus *Pentremites*, perhaps the best-known blastoid.

Encrinus

Crinoids

Primary Features

The 8 cm body or calyx is much wider than tall, made from a smal number of well-defined plates. The stem is stout and circular in section. The feathery arms are long, strongly plated and often found arranged in parallel.

Stratigraphy and Distribution

European Mid and Upper Triassic, such as the shelly limestones cr 'Muschelkalk' of Germany.

Additional Information

Encrinus was one of the last crinoids of the group Inadunata, in existence from the Lower Ordovician and comprising more than 200 species.

Similar Forms

The similar *Dadocrinus* is often found in the same sediments.

Encrinus could spread their arms to form a feeding fan.

Taxocrinus

Crinoids

Primary Features

A flexible, bag-like calyx 5–6 cm across, made from many small plates. The arms, flexibly attached to the calyx, are long and have several branches apiece. The mouth and food grooves are exposed on the upper surface of the calyx.

Stratigraphy and Distribution

Devonian-Lower Carboniferous of Europe and North America.

Additional Information

Taxocrinus and its relatives had a row of three 'infrabasal' plates at the base of the calyx, one plate smaller than the other two.

Similar Forms

Sagenocrinites from the Silurian of Europe and North America has a rigidly plated calyx 8–10 cm across. The arms are made from a single column of plates. Another similar form is *Protaxocrinus* from the Upper Ordovician (Ashgill).

Other Palaeozoic Crinoids

Crinoids

Platycrinites (**1**) has a rigid calyx 3–4 cm across, made of a small number of large plates. Each feathery arm consists of two rows of plates. The stem is flat and ribbon-like. Devonian-Carboniferous, Europe and North America.

Other Palaeozoic Crinoids

Crinoids

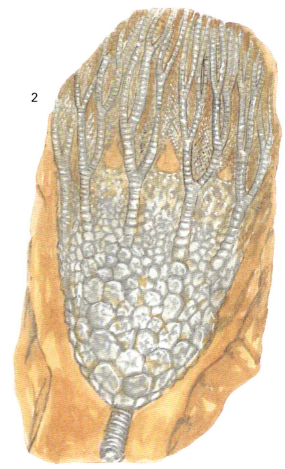

2

Scyphocrinites (2) has a calyx up to 15 cm across that subsumes the lower parts of the feathery arms. The mouth and food grooves are covered by plates. The stem ends with a balloon-like float called a lobolite. A good zone fossil for the Lowest Devonian, worldwide. Similar forms include the Lower Ordovician *Reteocrinites* and the strange *Barrandeocrinus* in which the arms drooped inwards over the calyx like a wilting daisy.

Pentacrinites

Crinoids

Primary Features

A very small, rigid calyx with long, feathery, flexible and many-branched arms. The stem is up to 1 m long and may have large side-branches or cirri that grow up to envelop the calyx.

Stratigraphy and Distribution

Triassic-Recent. Found as fossils in Europe and North America. Common in the English Lower Lias.

Additional Information

The plates of the stem in *Pentacrinites* are noteworthy for their distinctive star-shaped section.

Similar Forms

Other crinoids, although the stem plates are unmistakeable.

Pentacrinites are thought to have lived in colonies attached to floating driftwood.

Marsupites
Crinoids

Primary Features

Stemless, bud-shaped, globular calyx 2–3 cm across, made of a few large, sculptured plates which are pentagonal except for a ring of hexagonal plates round the middle. The arms are rarely found.

Stratigraphy and Distribution

Cretaceous (Senonian) of Europe and North America.

Additional Information

Marsupites is a free-living crinoid, a member of the same group that includes the modern feather-stars.

Similar Forms

Other small crinoids, especially if found without stems or arms.

Marsupites are made of pentagonal and hexagonal plates.

Uintacrinus

Crinoids

Primary Features

A stemless crinoid about the same size as a gooseberry. The calyx is made from many small polygonal plates. The long, strong, feathery arms originate from plates near the base of the calyx.

Stratigraphy and Distribution

Upper Cretaceous of Europe and North America.

Additional Information

A free-living crinoid, but of a very different form to the rigidly plated *Marsupites*.

Similar Forms

Other crinoids, especially if found without stems, but the origin of the arms low on the calyx in *Uintacrinus* is a distinctive feature.

Uintacrinus did not have stems, therefore were free-swimming crinoids.

Palaeocoma

Brittle-Stars

Primary Features

A brittle-star about 10 cm across with a tiny circular to pentagonal disc and very narrow, serpentine arms.

Stratigraphy and Distribution

Lower Jurassic (Lias) of Europe.

Additional Information

Brittle-stars have changed little in geological time. The Ordovician (Ashgill) *Lapworthura* looks much the same as the living *Ophiura*.

Similar Forms

Similar forms include *Encrinaster* with its long, narrow-tipped arms and pentagonal disc.

Upper Ordovician to Lower Carboniferous of Europe, especially the Lower Devonian Hunsrück shales of Germany.

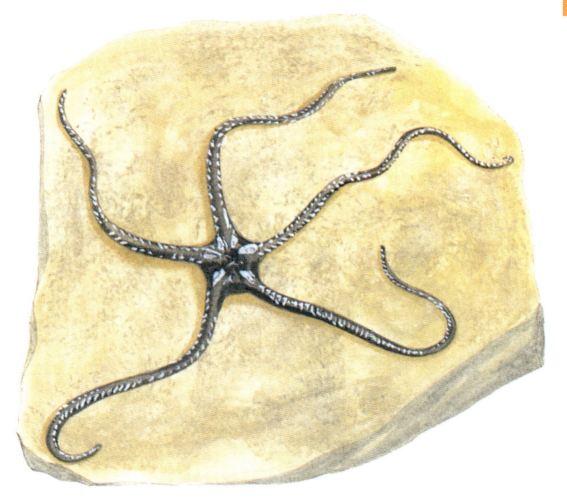

The brittle-star Palaeocoma used its arms as 'legs' to crawl across the sea floor.

Other Starfishes

Salteraster (**1**) is a true starfish 4–5 cm across. The large marginal plates on the broad, strong arms are separated from the dorsal plates by ribbons of flexible integument. Middle Ordovician-Silurian of Europe and North America. The similar *Siluraster* comes from the Ordovician of Britain and Bohemia.

Pentasteria (**2**) is a true starfish, 8–10 cm across, with a small body and narrow, straight arms with large plates on the margins and smaller inner plates. Jurassic-Eocene, Europe.

1

2

Other Starfishes

Metopaster (**3**) is a pentagon, 3–4 cm across, with extremely short arms but very prominent marginal plates. Upper Cretaceous (Maastrichtian).

Calliderma (**4**), 10–15 cm across, has a large body grading into short arms. Cretaceous–Oligocene, Europe.

3

4

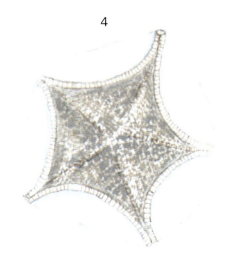

The Pentasteria is a true starfish fossil from the Jurassic-Eocene era.

Pygaster
Regular Echinoids

Primary Features

A sea-urchin with a rounded to pentagonal test about 6 cm across and 2–3 cm tall. There is a distinctive anal groove on the top surface.

Stratigraphy and Distribution

Jurassic-Cretaceous of Europe; common in the Bajocian (Middle Jurassic) of England.

Additional Information

Fossils may show small, circular marks that are the remnants of spine-bases.

Similar Forms

The Jurassic sea-urchin *Pedina* is similar except that the anus is less prominent.

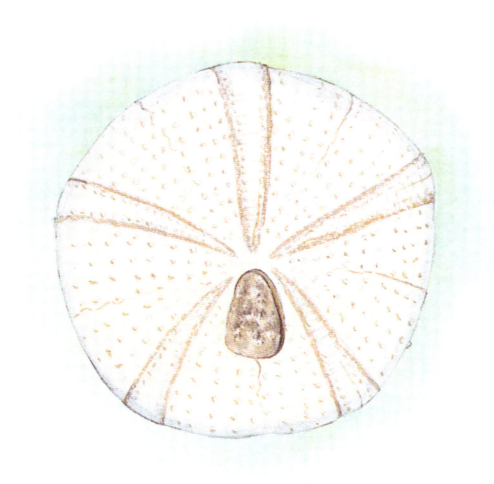

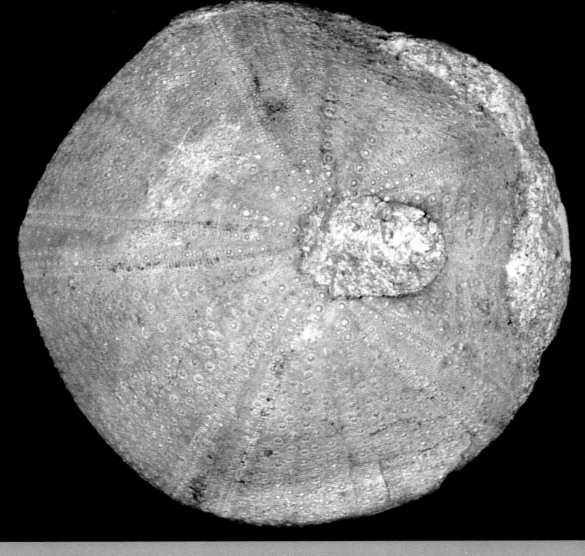

Pygaster have a distinctive anal groove on the top surface.

Acrosalenia

Regular Echinoids

Primary Features

A sea-urchin with a flattened test about 2 cm in diameter. Spine bases are prominent and warty, each one with a circle of smaller tubercles around the base.

Stratigraphy and Distribution

Jurassic-Cretaceous of Europe.

Additional Information

Although the presence of spines is evident in *Acrosalenia* and other echinoids, they are shed after death and found only rarely as fossils.

Similar Forms

Hemicidaris is slightly larger (3–4 cm), with a large mouth with notches around the edge and food grooves more sinuous and less well-defined than in *Acrosalenia*. Each spine-base tubercle has a circle of holes just below the tip.

The warty protuberances of the Acrosalenia are the remnants of spine bases.

Micraster

Irregular Echinoids

Primary Features

A heart urchin 4–6 cm long and 3–4 cm tall. The mouth is in the cleft at the top of the 'heart' protected by a lower 'lip'. The anus (at the other end) forms a swelling on the lower surface.

Stratigraphy and Distribution

Cretaceous (Cenomanian)-Palaeocene worldwide. Especially well known from Upper Cretaceous (Turonian-Senonian) of England and France.

Additional Information

Studies of the changes in shape in *Micraster* mapped through the Upper Cretaceous have revealed one of the classic case histories of evolution in action.

Similar Forms

A similar form is *Holaster* from the Jurassic and Cretaceous, in which the heart shape is not as marked as in *Micraster*.

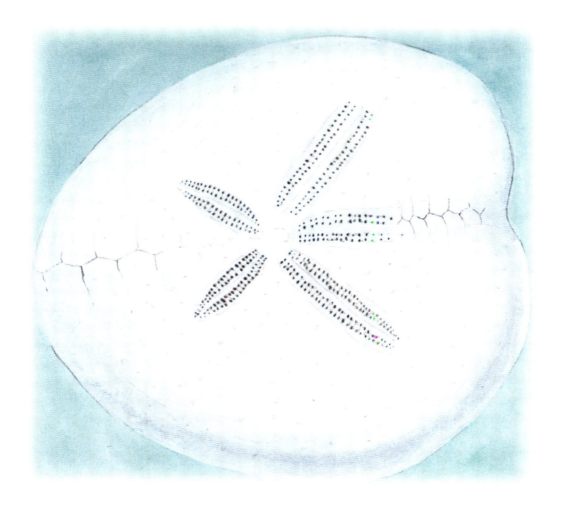

The changes in shape in Micraster have revealed evolution in action.

Other Irregular Echinoids

Conulus (**1**) is 4 cm across, 3–4 cm tall. Round in outline (although not perfectly circular), hemispherical to conical in side view. The mouth lies directly underneath the tall apex, with the anus on one edge. Cretaceous of the Northern Hemisphere, common in the English chalk (Senonian).

1

Other Irregular Echinoids

Clypeaster (2) is a flattened oval 11–12 cm long with broad, petal-shaped food grooves in the centre of the upper surface. The lower surface is flat or convex with the mouth in the centre and the anus on one edge. Eocene-Recent, worldwide; some species are useful Tertiary zone fossils. Similar forms include the Middle Jurassic *Nucleolites* about the same size and shape except that the food grooves run all the way round the test.

2

Clypeaster were relatively flat and are sometimes called 'sea biscuits'.

Mitrocystella

Calcichordates

Primary Features

Flattened echinoderm-like form with a distinct plated 'head' and short, segmented 'tail'. The plates on the upper surface are larger than those on the lower surface. More often found as fragments.

Stratigraphy and Distribution

Locally abundant in Ordovician shales of Brittany and Bohemia.

Additional Information

The irregular calcichordates occur in marine rocks from the Cambrian to the Devonian. Some scientists think that they are more closely related to vertebrates than echinoderms.

Similar Forms

Mitrocystites (Ordovician, Bohemia); *Placocystites* (Silurian, England);

Cothurnocystis (Ordovician, Scotland); *Ceratocystis* (Cambrian, Bohemia).

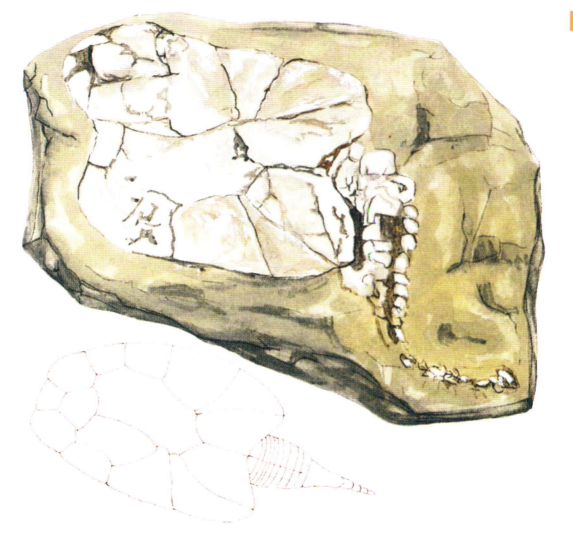

Monograptus

Primary Features

Monograptus (**1**). A uniserial, graptoloid form with thecae arranged along just one edge of the blade like hacksaw teeth. Colonies can be long and straight or arranged in graceful coils, and the thecal shape is similarly varied.

Stratigraphy and Distribution

Llandovery-Lower Devonian of Europe.

Additional Information

The various forms of *Monograptus* are extremely useful as zone fossils in the Silurian.

Similar Forms

Rastrites (Llandovery) has long, projecting thecae; *Cyrtograptus* (**2**; Wenlock, worldwide) is a beautiful, uniserial graptolite with branches thrown at regular intervals from the spiral main stem.

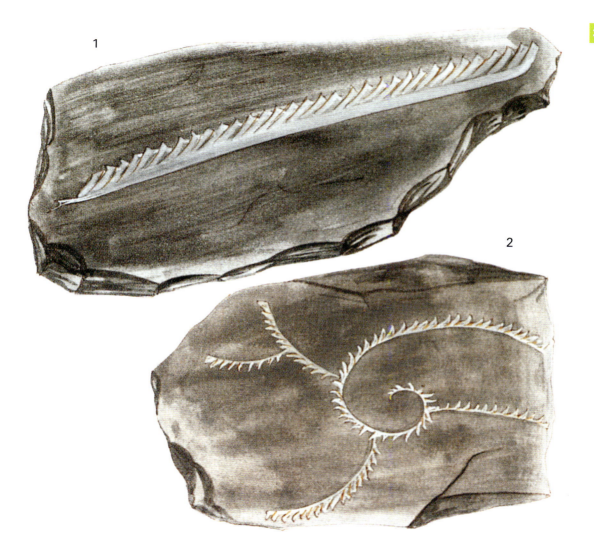

Monograptus are graptolites – the fossil remains of small colonial animals who were connected together by living tissue.

Tetragraptus

Primary Features

Tetragraptus (**1**) is a graptolite with four uniserial, fretsaw-like blades arranged in various ways according to the species, but always meeting at a central apex.

Stratigraphy and Distribution

Lower Ordovician (Arenig-Llanvirn), worldwide.

Additional Information

As with *Monograptus*, species of *Tetragraptus* can be useful as zone fossils.

Similar Forms

Phyllograptus (**2**; Lower Ordovician, worldwide) is made of four separate blades as in *Tetragraptus* but fused together back-to-back. The four blades (at right angles to one another) are usually only seen in specimens preserved in three dimensions.

Other Graptolites

Didymograptus (1), a graptolite with two uniserial branches, sometimes resembling a tuning fork in shape. Ordovician (Arenig-Carodoc), worldwide.

Diplograptus (2), leaf-like colonies with thecae facing outwards on both sides of the blade. Ordovician-Silurian (Llanvirn-Llandovery), worldwide. Similar forms include *Orthograptus* (Upper Ordovician-Lower Silurian) and *Climacograptus* (Arenig-Llandovery).

1

2

Other Graptolites

Dictyonema (3) is a finely branching, fan-like form with strong cross-branches between the main branches. Unlike most graptolites, which floated freely near the surface of the sea, the colonies of *Dictyonema* and its relatives were rooted to the seafloor. Middle Cambrian-Carboniferous, worldwide. Similar forms include *Rhabdinopora* (Tremadoc) although it may be confused with the bryozoan ***Fenestella***.

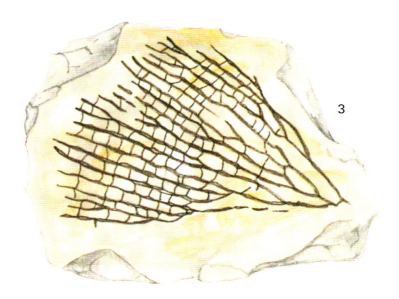

3

Didymograptus are tuning-fork shaped graptolites.

Cephalaspis

Jawless Fishes

Primary Features

An armoured fish, 10–20 cm long, with a broad, semicircular head, paddle-shaped fins behind and a slender, heavily armoured tail. Usually only isolated plates and scales are found.

Stratigraphy and Distribution

Silurian-Devonian of Eurasia and North America.

Additional Information

Ancient relatives of the modern lamprey, many different kinds of jawless fishes are known from the Upper Cambrian to the Devonian.

Similar Forms

Cephalaspis itself is fairly distinctive if found complete, but fragments may be confused with other forms such as *Pteraspis* (Silurian-Devonian).

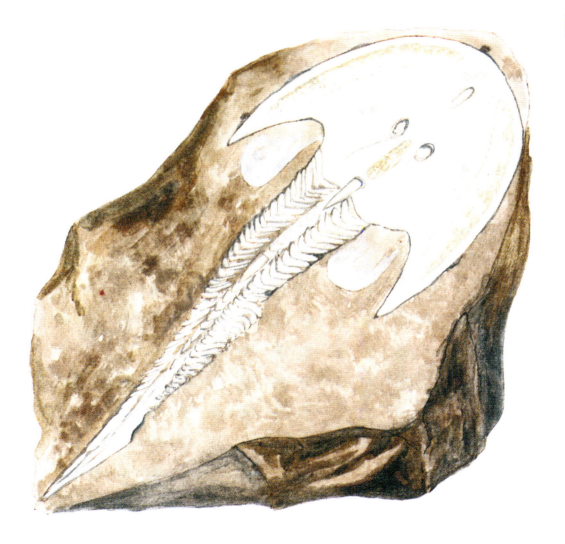

Placoderm Fishes

Pterichthyodes (1). A fish about 20 cm long with a heavy, box-like suit of armour and a scaly tail. The underside of the head armour is flat, but the upper surface is arched. Middle Devonian freshwater deposits, especially abundant in northern Scotland. Similar forms include *Bothriolepis* (Upper Devonian), armoured but with naked hindparts, the mid-Devonian *Asterolepis* and the unrelated ***Cephalaspis***.

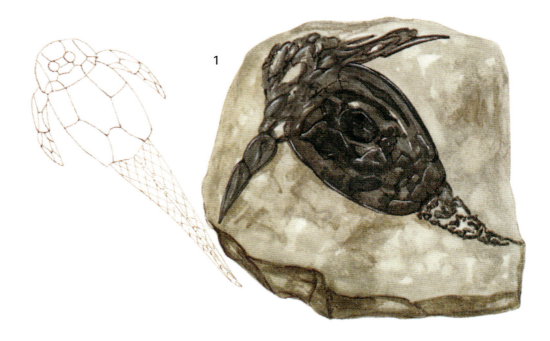

1

Placoderm Fishes

Coccosteus (**2**). A fish about 20 cm long with heavy body armour smoother in outline than in *Pterichthyodes* and more clearly divided into head and trunk sections. Another fish characteristic of the Middle Devonian of Scotland, although a number of highly varied relatives are known from the Upper Devonian of Germany.

2

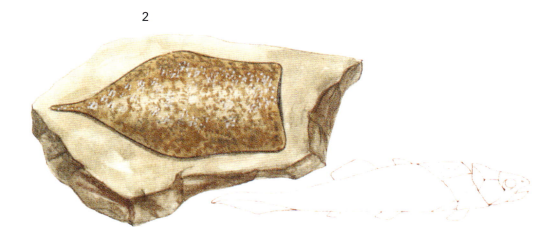

Sharks and Rays

Cartilaginous Fishes

Tooth of **Hybodus** (**1**). *Hybodus* represented a group of sharks common between the Triassic and Cretaceous. Their long (about 20 cm), fluted spines (**2**) were used to support the fins. Worldwide.

Sharks and Rays
Cartilaginous Fishes

Myliobatis (3). A ray with large batteries of teeth used for crushing shel fish. Cretaceous-Pliocene, worldwide. Shell-crushers from the Cretaceous shark *Ptychodus* have a distinctive, finger-print-like pattern of ridges.

The teeth of the shark *Lamna* (4) can be recognized by the two small accessory toothlets on either side of the pointed, main tooth. The large teeth of the great white shark *Carcharodon*, likewise known from Tertiary rocks around the world, are triangular and serrated without extra toothlets.

3

4

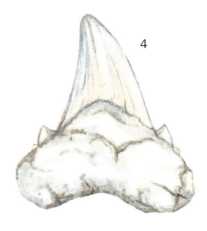

Dapedium
Bony Fishes

Primary Features

A deep-bodied, ray-finned fish about 25 cm long with a small mouth well-armed with stout peg-like teeth. The thick and shiny scales are square to rectangular or rhomboidal in shape.

Stratigraphy and Distribution

Lower Jurassic (Lias), familiar from Lyme Regis in Dorset, England.

Additional Information

Dapedium is a very early member of a group of fishes now almost entirely extinct, but for the heavily armoured garpike *Lepisosteus*, the bowfin *Amia* and a few other forms.

Similar Forms

The deep-bodied form has evolved many times in the history of fishes. Other examples include *Amphicentrum* (Carboniferous), *Cleithrolepsis* (Triassic) and *Microdon* (Jurassic).

Osteolepis
Bony Fishes

Primary Features

A small fish, 10–20 cm, with heavy scale armour. Often found complete or nearly so, *Osteolepis* and its close relatives have distinctive large scales or scutes on each side of the fin bases.

Stratigraphy and Distribution

Middle Devonian of northern Scotland. Similar forms are known from the Devonian of Europe, Canada, Spitzbergen, Greenland and Australia.

Additional Information

Osteolepis is a member of a group of lobe-finned fishes ancestral to the first amphibians, which appeared in the Upper Devonian.

Similar Forms

Similar forms include *Gyroptychius*, *Thursius*, *Glyptolepis* and the lungfish *Dipterus*.

Westlothiana

Reptiles

Primary Features

A lizard-like animal about 20 cm long with a small head, well-developed fore and hind limbs and a long, sinuous tail.

Stratigraphy and Distribution

Lower Carboniferous. So far known only from a single site at East Kirkton in southern Scotland.

Additional Information

Besides *Westlothiana*, affectionately known as 'Lizzie', East Kirkton has yielded fossils of amphibians and arthropods, opening a unique window on the Lower Carboniferous.

Similar Forms

Easily confused with the many contemporary species of Lower Carboniferous amphibian.

Ichthyosaur
Reptiles

Primary Features

The vertebrae (**1**) of these marine reptiles are circular, about 8 cm across (although size is extremely variable), slightly concave on each side and rather featureless except for swellings on the edges where other bones joined.

Stratigraphy and Distribution

Mesozoic, worldwide. The English Lias is noted for its ichthyosaur remains.

Additional Information

Ichthyosaurs were important marine reptiles that occupied the same ecological niche that dolphins and porpoises do today. Their pointed teeth (**2**) had deeply furrowed crowns.

Similar Forms

Vertebrae can be mistaken for those of other marine reptiles such as plesiosaurs. Large, pointed teeth (10 cm long) found isolated in Mesozoic sediments may come from large carnivorous plesiosaurs called pliosaurs.

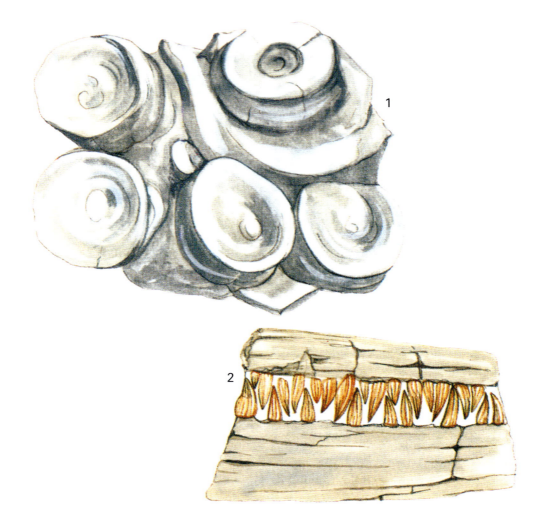

1

2

Seen here is a complete Icthyosaurus fossil, a reptilian marine animal comparable to today's dolphins.

Crocodiles

Reptiles

Primary Features

Crocodiles are betrayed as fossils by the square or rectangular bony plates (**1**) that formed their body armour. The honeycomb-like pitting on the top surfaces give them an appearance not dissimilar to waffles.

Stratigraphy and Distribution

Triassic-Recent, worldwide.

Additional Information

The pointed, curved and deeply rooted teeth (**2**) are also commonly found as fossils although their variation in size – even in one jaw – make them hard to identify to species.

Similar Forms

The pitted, bony plates or 'scutes' of crocodiles may be confused with the large, trapezium-shaped or rectangular scutes of tortoises such as *Trionyx* (Triassic-Recent, Old World) (**3**).

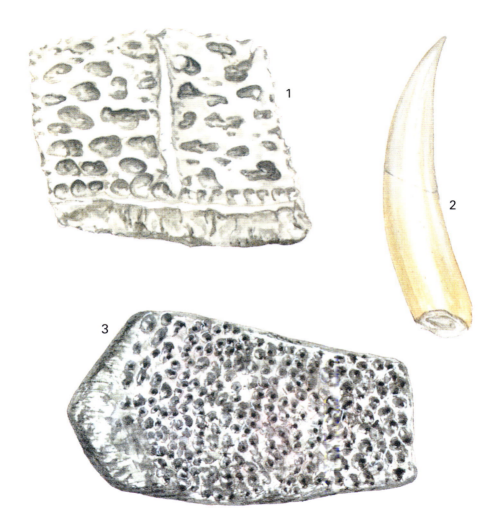

1

2

3

A complete crocodile fossil from the Jurassic era.

Iguanodon
Dinosaurs

Primary Features

Isolated bones such as this vertebra (**1**) and tall, flat-topped teeth (**2**) are mostly all that remains of the large plant-eating dinosaur *Iguanodon*.

Stratigraphy and Distribution

Lower Cretaceous of Europe (Neocomian), of western North America and Eastern Asia.

Additional Information

The first dinosaur to be described scientifically. Although the first known specimens were fragments, whole skeletons have been found in a mineshaft at Bernissart in Belgium.

Similar Forms

Most dinosaur specimens are found as small fragments of bones or teeth that may need specialized assistance for sure identification. The teeth of herbivores like *Iguanodon*, though, are easily distinguishable from the curved, serrated teeth of carnivores such as *Megalosaurus*.

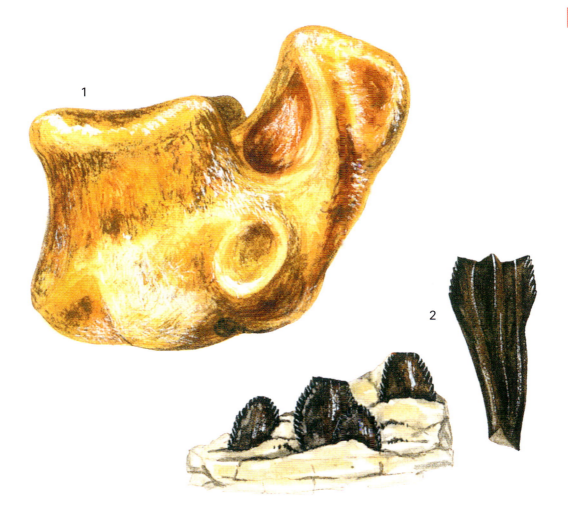

Baryonyx

Dinosaurs

Primary Features

An unusual 10 m-long dinosaur with a large, flat crocodile-like head full of sharp teeth and impressive 30 cm scimitar-like claws on its forefeet. It is thought to have dined on fish.

Stratigraphy and Distribution

Lower Cretaceous, England.

Additional Information

The first specimen was discovered by chance by an enthusiast out walking his dog – proof that great fossils await discovery by the amateur.

Similar Forms

Similar forms may occur in the Cretaceous of West Africa.

Dinosaur Eggs
Dinosaurs

Primary Features

Dinosaur eggs are usually found as fragments and are difficult to identify. Very occasionally, entire buried nests of the eggs, looking like very old, dried potatoes, are found in circular or linear arrangements.

Stratigraphy and Distribution

Mesozoic, especially Upper Cretaceous sediments of southern France and Transylvania.

Additional Information

The species of dinosaur that laid any particular egg is of course impossible to determine, but a favourite candidate for French eggs is the large, plant-eating dinosaur *Hypselosaurus*.

Similar Forms

None.

A nest of Protoceratops dinosaur eggs discovered in Outer Mongolia.

Ice-Age Mammal Teeth

Mammals

Equus; horse molars (**1**) are tall and rather square in section, with a distinctive pattern of loops and contours when seen in top view (**2**). Pleistocene river gravels.

Bison; the lower molars (**3**) of the steppe bison *Bison priscus* are tall and blade-like; the upper teeth are more blocky in appearance. The teeth of the extinct wild cattle *Bos primigenius* look very similar, but have taller crowns. Both are found in Pleistocene river gravels and cave sites.

Crocuta; cave hyena canines (**4**) have a distinctive, pointed shape. Teeth of bear *Ursus* are similar in shape but larger. Mostly found in ancient 'hyena dens' in caves, where they can occur in abundance.

1

2

3

Ice-Age Mammal Teeth

Mammals

Mammuthus; the numerous and close-packed enamel ridges of the huge, heavy teeth of the woolly mammoth (**5**) help to distinguish the teeth from those of related elephants such as *Palaeoloxodon* and *Archidiskodon*, which have fewer ridges, more widely spaced. Found in glacial and river gravels, and even occasionally dredged up from the North Sea in fishing nets!

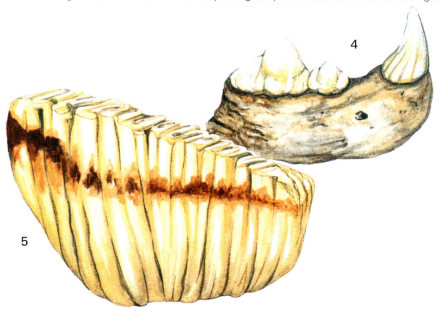

4

5

These Mammuthus teeth display the close-packed ridges characteristic of these fossils.

Hominid Tools

Mammals

Acheulean hand-axe (1), the classic stone tool. Invented by *Homo erectus*, this Swiss Army Knife of the Stone Age remained part of the human toolkit for more than 500,000 years.

Mousterian flakes and scraper (2) represent the culture of Neanderthal Man (*Homo sapiens neanderthalensis*) in western Europe.

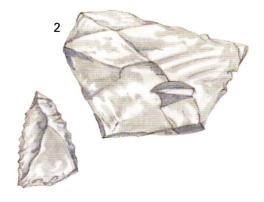

Hominid Tools

Mammals

Cave paintings such as this bison (3) are rare but telling evidence for the arrival of *Homo sapiens* in Europe. The most famous cave paintings, including this one, are at Lascaux in the Dordogne valley in south-west France.

3

A scraper, used by early *Homo sapiens*.

Further Reading

Bonewitz, R.L., *Rock & Gem: The Definitive Guide to Rocks, Minerals, Gemstones and Fossils*, Dorling Kindersley Publishers Ltd, 2005

Davis, P. and Kenrick, P., *Fossil Plants (Living Past)*, The Natural History Museum, 2004

Fortey, R., *Fossils: The Key to the Past*, Stationery Office Books, 1991

Hamilton, W.R., Woolley, A.R. and Bishop, A.C., *Philip's Guide to Minerals, Rocks and Fossils*, Philip's, 1999

Ivanov, M., Hrdlickova, S. and Gregorova, R., *The Complete Enyclopedia of Fossils*, Rebo Intl, 2003

Lichter, G., *Fossil Collector's Handbook: Finding, Identifying, Preparing, Displaying*, Sterling, 1994

Maisey, J., *Discovering Fossil Fishes*, Westview, 2000

Milsom, C. and Rigby, S., *Fossils at a Glance*, Blackwell Science Ltd, 2003

Morgan, B., *Rock & Fossil Hunter*, Dorling Kindersley Publishers Ltd, 2005

Natural History Museum, *The British Mesozoic Fossils*, Intercept Ltd, 2001

Natural History Museum, *The British Palaeozoic Fossils*, Intercept Ltd, 2002

Palmer, D., *Fossils (Collins GEM)*, Collins, 2006

Parker, S., *The World Encyclopedia of Fossils and Fossil Collecting*, Lorenz Books, 2007

Pellant, C. and Pellant, H., *Fossils: A Photographic Field Guide*, New Holland Publishers Ltd, 2007

Taylor, P.D., *Fossil (Eyewitness Guide)*, Dorling Kindersley Publishers Ltd, 2003

Taylor, P.D. and Lewis, D.N., *Fossil Invertebrates*, The Natural History Museum, 2005

Thompson, K., *Fossils: A Very Short Introduction*, Oxford University Press, 2005

Toghill, P., *The Geology of Britain*, The Crowood Press Ltd, 2002

Ward, D., *DK Handbook: Fossils*, Dorling Kindersley Publishers Ltd, 2000

Westwood, R., *Fossils and Rocks of the Jurassic Coast*, Inspiring Places Publishing, 2006

Picture Credits

Corbis: James L. Amos: 56–57; DK Limited: 32–33, 74–75, 84–85, 198–99, 240–41, 290–91, 298–99, 306–07, 310–11; Kevin Schafer: 314–15, 362–63.

GeoScience Features Picture Library: 50–51, 60–61, 212–13, 232–33, 236–37, 370–71; D. Bayliss (RIDA): 36–37, 64–65, 70–71, 92–93, 96–97, 100–01, 104–05, 108–09, 112–13, 118–19, 122–23, 126–27, 130–31, 138–39, 144–45, 148–49, 152–53, 158–59, 162–63, 180–81, 186–87, 202–03, 220–21, 246–47, 254–55, 258–59, 270–71, 330–31, 342–43, 358–59, 378–79; Dr B. Booth: 88–89, 134–35, 170–71, 216–17, 226–27, 250–51, 266–67, 274–75, 280–81, 318–19, 322–23, 374–75; D. Boyd: 40–41, 174–75; M. Land: 46–47, 166–67, 194–95, 208–09, 302–03, 326–27, 336–37.

Index and Checklist

All species in Roman type are illustrated.

Keep a record of your sightings by ticking the boxes.